PREPARE FOR SQE

FLK1 PRACTICE ASSESSMENT

180 SQE1-STYLE QUESTIONS WITH ANSWERS

Editor: Mark Thomas

Series editors: Amy Sixsmith and David Sixsmith

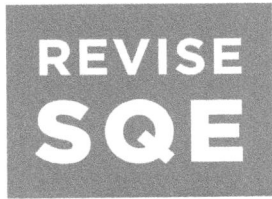

First published in 2023 by Fink Publishing Ltd

Impression number 10 9 8 7 6 5 4

British Library Cataloguing in Publication Data
A catalogue record for this book is available from the British Library
ISBN: 9781914213441

This book is also available in various ebook formats.
Ebook ISBN: 9781914213458

Cover and text design by BMLD (bmld.uk)
Production and typesetting by Westchester Publishing Services UK
Development editing by Llinos Edwards

Fink Publishing Ltd
E-mail: hello@revise4law.co.uk
www.revise4law.co.uk

Contents

This practice assessment was designed in accordance with the SQE Assessment Specification published in April 2023 which came into force from 1 September 2023.

Contributors

■ THE EDITOR

Mark Thomas is a practising barrister and has taught law for several years at both undergraduate and postgraduate levels, including the Legal Practice Course. Mark has published academic textbooks in the field of criminal law and evidence, and has extensive experience in writing revision-style books for law students. He is also the co-author of *Revise SQE: Criminal Law* and *Revise SQE: Criminal Practice* and editor of *Revise SQE: Ethics and Professional Conduct*, and acts as the multiple-choice question (MCQ) advisor and reviewer for the Revise SQE series.

Mark is the author of MCQs on ethics and professional conduct for this volume.

■ MCQ AUTHORS

Revise SQE would like to thank the following for their contribution of MCQs to this book:

- Business law and practice: Stephanie Jones, senior lecturer at the University of Central Lancashire
- Contract law: Ryan Murray, principal lecturer at Nottingham Law School, Nottingham Trent University
- Dispute resolution: David Sixsmith, assistant professor at Northumbria Law School
- The legal system of England and Wales and legal services: Amy Sixsmith, senior lecturer at the University of Sunderland
- Tort law: Linda Chadderton, senior lecturer at the University of Central Lancashire.

Revise SQE would also like to thank Benjamin Jones, University of South Wales, for his assistance in reviewing MCQs for FLK1.

■ SERIES EDITORS

Amy Sixsmith is a senior lecturer in law at the University of Sunderland and a senior fellow of the Higher Education Academy.

David Sixsmith is assistant professor at Northumbria Law School and a senior fellow of the Higher Education Academy.

Introduction

Welcome to *Prepare for SQE1: FLK1 Practice Assessment*. We are proud to present this book as a companion to our *Revise SQE* series of revision guides. In this book, we aim to continue our goal of assisting you in preparing for and passing the Solicitors Qualifying Examination (SQE1).

This introductory section will explain how the book is structured, and offers practical advice on preparing for your SQE1 assessment, how to approach multiple-choice questions (MCQs) and what to expect on the day of the assessment. An assessment briefing follows, which is designed to get you into the mindset for sitting these SQE1-style MCQs.

We then present 180 SQE1-style MCQs, written by our expert team of *Revise SQE* authors. The MCQs are presented, as far as possible, in the same style and format as that adopted in the SQE1 assessments. The MCQs will be broken down into two sessions, each consisting of 90 MCQs (180 in total).

At the end of each session, we offer you the opportunity to reflect on your progress/performance. By honestly reflecting on your experience, you will be in a better position to consider whether you are ready to sit the SQE1 assessments.

You will then be provided with detailed answers to the MCQs for each session, including a summary sheet for easy cross-reference. You will be able to understand why each option was correct or incorrect. Where appropriate or relevant, the answers will refer to legal authorities assessable in SQE1, and link to our series of *Revise SQE* books and associated chapters.

At the end of this book, you are provided with some final words of advice and a list of Frequently Asked Questions (FAQs) on the SQE1 assessments.

We hope that you find this book to be a useful resource in your preparations for SQE1, and we wish you the very best of luck in your assessments.

■ THE SQE1 ASSESSMENTS
Below is a summary of the SQE1 assessments.

ASSESSMENT BREAKDOWN
The SQE consists of SQE1 and SQE2. The SQE1 assessment is broken down into two components:
- Functioning legal knowledge (FLK) 1, and
- Functioning legal knowledge (FLK) 2.

You must achieve the necessary pass mark in *both* FLK1 and FLK2 to pass SQE1 as a whole. If you fail either FLK1 or FLK2, you are only required to resit the assessment that you failed.

You must pass both SQE1 and SQE2 in order to apply to become a solicitor.

How the assessments are structured

Each FLK assessment for SQE1 consists of 180 single best answer MCQs (360 in total). Each question will have five possible answers, but only one answer that is considered to be correct. This correct answer will score a mark of 1 if you choose it. All other responses, including where multiple responses are recorded, will be awarded a score of 0. No negative marking is used in the SQE1 assessments (ie, no marks are deducted for incorrect responses).

Your total score is a percentage based on the proportion of correct responses across the assessment.

If you are undertaking an SQE-preparation course, you may be used to sitting practice assessments within a particular FLK subject matter (eg, dispute resolution). You may have, therefore, had the opportunity to revise and prepare for MCQs on a single FLK subject. However:
- The FLK1 assessment will not identify the topic or subject matter of the MCQ: that is for you to determine.
- The assessment will not group MCQs according to the FLK subject matter: all MCQs will be randomly distributed across the two sessions in FLK1.

This book also adopts this approach, to provide you with a more realistic simulation of the FLK1 assessment.

Assessment sessions

Table 1 provides a breakdown of the SQE1 assessment sessions and timings.

Table 1: SQE1 assessment sessions and timings

Assessment	Timings
FLK1 assessment day	Session 1: Answer 90 MCQs (2 hrs 33 mins) – Break for 1 hour Session 2: Answer 90 MCQs (2 hrs 33 mins)
FLK2 assessment day (4 days later)	Session 1: Answer 90 MCQs (2 hrs 33 mins) – Break for 1 hour Session 2: Answer 90 MCQs (2 hrs 33 mins)

Answering 90 MCQs within 2 hours 33 minutes allows *1 minute, 42 seconds per question,* under exam conditions. Of course, some questions will take more or less time to answer than others.

Please take a moment to think about that: on average, within 1 minute and 42 seconds you will have to:
- read the MCQ, including the various answers
- distil from that MCQ what the question is assessing
- work out which of the five possible answers is the correct (or 'single best') answer.

This will be an intensive assessment. You must ensure that you are properly prepared for it, in terms of your subject knowledge and also your mental resilience and time management.

THE FLK1 ASSESSMENT SPECIFICATION

This practice assessment book will prepare you for FLK1. According to the SQE1 Assessment Specification, the following will be assessed on FLK1:
- Business law and practice
- Dispute resolution
- Contract

- Tort
- Legal system of England and Wales
- Constitutional and administrative law and EU law
- Legal services.

However, please note:
- The principles of taxation will also be examined, but only in the context of business law and practice for FLK1.
- Ethics and professional conduct will be examined pervasively across the assessment.

Law at the time of the assessment

The cut-off date for the law upon which candidates are examined in the SQE will be *four calendar months* prior to the date of the first assessment in an assessment window. You will not be tested on the development of the law.

FLK blueprint

The Solicitors Regulation Authority (SRA) has provided a 'blueprint' for the FLK subjects, which identifies the percentage of each topic within the FLK assessment. Table 2 outlines the SRA's blueprint for FLK1 and the approach adopted in this book regarding the number of MCQs per FLK subject.

Table 2: Blueprint of FLK1

FLK1	Potential percentage of MCQs in FLK1	Number of MCQs in this book
Business organisations, rules and procedures, including taxation of business organisations	14–20%	28
The principles, procedures and processes involved in dispute resolution	14–20%	28
Core principles of contract law	14–20%	28
Core principles of tort	14–20%	28
The legal system of England and Wales, Sources of law constitutional and administrative law, EU law	14–20%	28
Legal services	12–16%	23
Ethics and professional conduct	'pervades'	17

We believe that allocating this number of MCQs per FLK1 subject in this book is the best possible approach to assist you in your SQE1 preparation. However, please be aware that:
- The real FLK1 assessment may not be so balanced.
- FLK1 MCQs may draw on any combination of the subject areas that may be encountered in practice (eg, a dispute resolution MCQ may require an understanding of contract law and legal services).

You cannot, therefore, compartmentalise your understanding of the FLK1 subject matter; you must have a working knowledge of all FLK subjects and how they interact.

Further help from Revise SQE

- Our series of *Revise SQE* books covers each FLK subject.
- A *Revise SQE Checklist* is available for each FLK1 subject, which shows the SQE1 Assessment Specification in full and the corresponding *Revise SQE* books and chapters. This checklist is available at revise4law.co.uk/books/.

- A guide on the legal authorities that candidates must be able to recall or recite as part of the FLK1 assessment (eg, *Rylands v Fletcher* in tort) has been produced by the team at Revise SQE and is available at revise4law.co.uk/books/table-of-legal-authorities/.
- Visit revise4law.co.uk/legal-updates/ for regular updates relating to the law assessable in SQE1. These updates identify how the law has been impacted or changed, and the assessment period relating to that update.

■ PREPARING FOR SINGLE BEST ANSWER MCQS

For SQE1 assessment, MCQs are designed to allow you to demonstrate the competence required and expected of a newly qualified solicitor (a 'day one' solicitor).

WHAT IS A SINGLE BEST ANSWER MCQ?

Single best answer MCQs are a specialised form of question, used extensively in other fields such as in training medical professionals. The idea behind single best answer MCQs is that each option might look equally attractive, sharing commonalities and correct statements of law or principle, but only one option is absolutely correct (in the sense that it is the 'best' answer). Traditional MCQs usually feature distractors (other possible answers) that are implausible and therefore obviously wrong, but in a well-constructed single best answer MCQ, different options will contain some similarities and also subtle differences. Your skill will be to identify which, out of the options provided, is the single best answer.

HOW ARE SINGLE BEST ANSWER MCQS STRUCTURED?

For SQE1, single best answer MCQs will be structured as follows:

A woman is charged with battery, having thrown a rock towards another person intending to scare them. The rock hits the person in the head, causing no injury. The woman claims that she never intended that the rock hit the person, but the prosecution allege that the woman was reckless as to whether the rock would hit the other person.

Which of the following is the most accurate statement regarding the test for recklessness in relation to a battery?

A. There must have been a risk that force would be applied by the rock, and that the reasonable person would have foreseen that risk and unjustifiably taken it.
B. There must have been a risk that force would be applied by the rock, and that the woman should have foreseen that risk and unjustifiably taken it.
C. There must have been a risk that force would be applied by the rock, and that the woman must have foreseen that risk and unjustifiably taken it.
D. There must have been a risk that force would be applied by the rock, and that both the woman and the reasonable person should have foreseen that risk and unjustifiably taken it.
E. There must have been a risk that force would be applied by the rock, but there is no requirement that the risk be foreseen.

The factual scenario.
First, you will be provided with a factual scenario that sets the scene for the question to be asked.

The stem.
Next, you will be provided with the question that you must find the single best answer to.

The possible answers.
Finally, you will be provided with **five** possible answers. There is only one single best answer that must be chosen. The other answers, known as 'distractors', are not the 'best' answer available.

HOW DO I TACKLE SINGLE BEST ANSWER MCQS?

No exact art exists in terms of answering single best answer MCQs; success depends on your subject knowledge and understanding of how to apply it to the question scenario. Despite this, the following tips and tricks might be helpful.

1 Read the question twice	2. Understand the question being asked	3. Select the answer if you know it outright	4. If not, employ a process of elimination	5. Take an educated and reasoned guess	6. Skip and come back to it later

1. Read the entire question at least twice

This sounds obvious but is so often overlooked. You are advised to read the entire question once, taking in all relevant pieces of information, understanding what the question is asking you and being aware of the options available. Once you have done that, read the entire question again and this time pay careful attention to the wording that is used.

- In the factual scenario: Does it use any words that stand out? Do any words used have legal bearing? What are you told, and what are you not told?
- In the stem: What are you being asked? Are there certain words to look out for (eg 'should', 'must', 'will', 'shall')?
- In the possible answers: What are the differences between each option? Are they substantial or subtle differences? Do any differences turn on a word or a phrase?

You should be prepared to give each question at least two viewings to mitigate any misunderstandings or oversights.

2 Understand the question being asked

It is important first that you understand what the question is asking of you. The SQE1 assessment specification has identified that the FLK assessments may consist of single best answer MCQs that, for example:

- require you to simply identify a correct legal principle or rule
- require you not only to identify the correct legal principle or rule, but also to apply that principle or rule to the factual scenario
- provide the correct legal principle or rule, but require you to identify how it should be properly applied and/or the outcome of that proper application.

By identifying what the question is seeking you to do, you can then understand what it is testing, and how to approach the available answers.

3. Select the answer if you know it outright

You may feel as though a particular answer 'jumps out' at you, and that you are certain it is correct. It is very likely that the answer is correct. Whilst you should be confident in your answers, do not allow your confidence (and perhaps overconfidence) to rush you into making a decision. Review all of the options one final time before you move on to the next question.

4. Employ a process of elimination if you do not know the answer outright

There may be situations in which the answer is not obvious from the outset. This may be due to the close similarities between different answers. Remember, it is the 'single best answer' that you are looking for. If you keep this in mind, it will be easier to employ a process of elimination. Identify which answers you are sure are *not* correct (or not the 'best') and whittle down your options. Once you have only two options remaining, carefully scrutinise the wording used in both answers and look back to the question being asked. Identify what you consider to be the best answer, in light of that question. Review your answer and move on to the next question.

5. Take an educated and reasoned guess

There may be circumstances, quite commonly, in which you do not know the answer to the question. If this happens, try as hard as you can to eliminate any distractors that you are positive are incorrect, and then take an educated and reasoned guess based on the other options available.

6. Skip and come back to it later

If time permits, you might think it appropriate to skip a question that you are unsure of and return to it before the end of the assessment. If you do so, we would advise:

• that you make a note of what question you have skipped or click 'Flag for review' on your screen, and
• ensure you leave sufficient time for you to go back to that question before the end of the assessment.

The same advice applies to any question that you have answered but for which you remain unsure.

■ ON THE DAY

The following provides a brief summary of what to expect on the day of the assessment. For further information, see the SQE section of the SRA's website (sqe.sra.org.uk).

A number of FAQs are provided at the end of this book, which may assist you with some queries you have about the assessment on the day.

THE TEST CENTRE

The FLK1 assessment will take place in a Pearson VUE test centre. These test centres are located across the country.

After you book your assessments, the SRA will send you an email for each assessment day, confirming the time at which you must report to the assessment centre, the location and duration of your assessment.

If you are late for the time specified, you will not be permitted entry into the assessment.

SECURITY CHECKS AND THE ASSESSMENT ROOM

When you arrive at the Pearson VUE test centre, you will complete registration, including an ID check (see FAQs on **page 151** for more on ID checks).

Following the security checks, you will then be seated at a computer desk, where you will be required to:
• complete a Fit to Sit declaration
• confirm that you accept the Candidate Confidentiality Policy and the Assessment Regulations.

You must not have any personal belongings with you during the assessment, which includes food and water. Should you require water, you must leave the assessment room (though see below for further information about unscheduled breaks).

You will be provided with an erasable whiteboard notepad and marker pen to be used only during the assessment. These must be handed in at the end of the assessment.

THE CONDUCT OF THE ASSESSMENT

You will sit the SQE1 assessments on a computer in the Pearson Vue test centre. The following will be displayed on each display screen that sets out a question:
- a timer – indicating the time remaining within the session
- a question counter – setting out how many questions are in the session and the number of the question you are answering (eg 8 of 90)
- a calculator icon – this can be selected to bring up the online calculator
- a flag – this can be selected to mark a question for review.

Each MCQ will also feature a tick box, allowing you to choose your answer to that particular question.

SCHEDULED AND UNSCHEDULED BREAKS

Following Session 1, you are provided with a 1-hour break (a 'scheduled break') in which you must leave the assessment room. You may retrieve personal belongings at this time.

You are advised to return after 50 minutes to engage with security checks and be seated at your desk.

You are permitted to leave the assessment room during the assessment (an 'unscheduled break') in order to use the toilet, have a drink of water, eat or obtain medication. However, the assessment timer is not stopped for unscheduled breaks (ie, the timer continues to run).

You are not permitted to leave the assessment room for any other reason, or to leave the assessment early.

COMPLETING THE ASSESSMENT

Once you have completed your assessment, you will be escorted from the assessment room and will be permitted to leave the test centre. Please see **page 149** for information relating to your results.

◼ HOW BEST TO USE THIS BOOK

Prepare for SQE1: FLK1 Practice Assessment has been designed, in so far as is possible, to replicate the assessments you will be faced with for SQE1. In particular, the structure and style of the MCQs in this book attempt to replicate the display screen in the real examination.

ACHIEVING A SIMILAR EXPERIENCE

You should try to sit these MCQs in a timed, closed-book fashion, to replicate the experience of the real SQE1 assessments. To assist with ensuring a similar experience, you are advised to have the following equipment with you:
- Pencil/pen – you could complete the assessment in pencil, so that you can look over your responses should time permit and change your answers.
- Paper – if you do not wish to write in the book.

- Calculator – a mobile phone will be sufficient for this.
- Stopwatch – on a mobile phone will be sufficient; but do not use your mobile for any other purpose. (You are *not* permitted to take a mobile phone or any materials other than those provided to you by the test centre into the real SQE1 assessment.)

We have listed the possible answers to each question A–E in this book, to assist you when it comes to reviewing the answers at the end of the assessment. This approach is also beneficial if you do not wish to write in the book. Note however that the SQE1 MCQs will not feature letters at the start of each answer.

Make use of the 'Flag for review' on each question too: circle the flag if you need to come back to a particular MCQ at a later time.

ANSWERS

Once you have answered all 180 MCQs, you will have the opportunity to review the answers to those MCQs, including an explanation as to why a particular answer was the single best choice. Please do not be tempted to read ahead and view the answers before or during the assessment. Treat this simulated SQE-style assessment as if you were sitting the real SQE1 assessment.

FURTHER PREPARATION

The SQE website offers candidates the opportunity to experience a simulation of the exam, including sample questions and a realistic user interface. Make sure that you visit the SQE section of the SRA website to try out the exam functionality.

■ FINAL WORDS

We hope that you find this practice assessment book helpful in your preparation for SQE1. Before attempting any MCQs, please read through the Assessment briefing on the opposite page.

Assessment briefing

■ CANDIDATE INSTRUCTIONS

Prepare for SQE1: FLK1 Practice Assessment will follow, as far as possible, the format that the SQE1 MCQs will be presented on a computer screen. On the test day, candidates are given guidance about the test via a tutorial, which is viewed before the test begins. This does not form part of your testing time.

Before you attempt the MCQs that follow, you are strongly advised to do the following:
- Choose a date and time when you are able to dedicate the time required to complete this simulated SQE-style assessment.
- Find a suitably quiet location to complete the practice assessment.

This book has been specifically written to replicate the SQE1 assessment environment that you will face at the test centre. Use this opportunity to prepare for that element of the assessment as well.

■ ASSESSMENT DURATION

Before you sit Session 1, please ensure that you have set a timer for 2 hours, 33 minutes. This is the maximum amount of time you will have to answer the questions.

■ PERMITTED MATERIALS

SQE1 is a closed-book assessment. This means that you are not permitted any materials during the assessment. We advise that you do not use any resources or materials whilst attempting this practice assessment. This will help to give you a more accurate indication of whether you are ready to sit SQE1.

In the SQE1 assessment, your display screen will feature a calculator. You are, therefore, permitted the use of a calculator in this practice assessment.

■ READY TO BEGIN?

Once you are ready to commence Session 1 of *Prepare for SQE1: FLK1 Practice Assessment*, click the start button on your timer and begin (questions on the next page).

Session 1 questions

Flag for review 🏴

Two companies are locked in a contractual dispute over non-performance. Proceedings have been issued and a stay of proceedings has been ordered to enable the parties to attempt alternative dispute resolution (ADR). The opponent proposes mediation. However, the client, who is the claimant in the matter, responds to the proposal and refuses to engage in mediation, citing the opponent's alleged history of non-performance as a reason for not trusting the opponent to engage in the mediation process. The case proceeds to trial and the client is successful in the action.

Which of the following best describes how the court will likely deal with the legal costs of the action and why?

A. The court will likely order that the opponent pay the client's legal costs in full as the client's allegations of the opponent's non-performance of the contract has been proved. The client was therefore fully justified in their distrust of the opponent's offer to mediate. ☐

B. The court will likely order that the opponent pay the client's legal costs in full as the client has been successful in the action overall, applying the principle that costs follow the event. ☐

C. The court will order that the client pay the opponent's legal costs in full, as the client has unreasonably refused to engage in mediation. ☐

D. The court will order that the client pay a percentage of the opponent's legal costs as well as their own by way of sanction for unreasonably refusing to mediate. ☐

E. The court will order that the opponent pay a percentage of the client's legal costs as well as their own as they made a genuine offer to mediate. ☐

Q2 of 90   Flag for review 🏴

A woman advertises her car for sale. A man sees the advertisement and comes to inspect the car. The woman then agrees to sell the car to the man for the sum of £8,000. The market value of the car is £15,000.

The man pays a deposit of £2,000 and agrees to pay the remainder when he collects the car the next day. Later that evening, the woman contacts the man and tells him that she received a higher offer by a third party and will not sell the car to the man for £8,000.

Which of the following best describes the legal position?

A. The woman is bound to sell the car to the third party, as the third party has offered the higher amount overall.

B. The woman is bound to sell the car to the man, as the man has provided sufficient consideration in exchange for the woman's promise to sell for £8,000.

C. The woman is not bound to sell the car to the man, as the sum of £8,000 is insufficient as consideration as it is significantly less than the market value of the car.

D. The woman is not bound to sell the car to the man, as she is not required to keep her offer open and can withdraw it at any time.

E. The woman is not bound to sell the car to the man, as the payment of £2,000 made by the man will be regarded as past consideration.

Q3 of 90   Flag for review 🏴

A solicitor is authorised to provide legal services by the Solicitors Regulation Authority (SRA). The solicitor works on a freelance basis.

Which of the following statements best describes the solicitor's authorisation to carry on reserved legal activities?

A. The solicitor may carry on all reserved legal activities.

B. The solicitor may carry on all reserved legal activities, except the exercise of a right of audience.

C. The solicitor cannot provide reserved legal activities because they are working on a freelance basis.

D. The solicitor may carry on all reserved legal activities, except notarial activities.

E. The solicitor may carry on all reserved legal activities, except notarial activities, providing the solicitor's organisation is registered as a sole practice or they provide any reserved legal activities through an authorised body.

Flag for review 🏳

The claimant is cycling through a busy city centre when the defendant, driving a delivery van, reverses from a shop forecourt into the claimant, knocking them to the ground and causing the claimant personal injury. The claimant is not wearing a bicycle helmet and suffers fractures to the head, ribs and arms.

Which of the following is likely to be the court's view when considering whether the claimant has contributed to their injury?

A. The court will likely find the defendant 100% at fault as the onus is on the defendant, as the reversing driver, to ensure the road is clear. ☐

B. The court will likely find the defendant 100% at fault as the claimant, as a cyclist, has the right of way. ☐

C. The court will likely find the defendant primarily liable but reduce the claimant's damages by 50% for failing to heed the presence of the defendant's delivery van. ☐

D. The court will likely find the defendant primarily liable but reduce the claimant's damages by 100% to represent the injuries that would not have occurred had the claimant been wearing a helmet. ☐

E. The court will likely find the defendant primarily liable but reduce the claimant's damages to reflect the claimant's failure to take reasonable care of their own safety. ☐

Flag for review 🏳

A client, a building firm, is engaged in a dispute worth £290,000 with a sub-contractor. Whilst the dispute is ongoing, the client is unable to continue the work needed to complete the project, which is having a substantial adverse impact on the client's financial position. The parties are entrenched in their respective positions with early negotiations showing no sign of potential agreement.

Which of the following is the client's best option for resolving the dispute and why?

A. Arbitration, as it is in the client's best interests to have a decision imposed upon them that brings the dispute to a conclusion as quickly as possible. ☐

B. Arbitration, as it is best that a confidential decision is imposed on the parties. ☐

C. Mediation, as it is quicker and will mean that working relations between the parties will be preserved once the dispute has concluded. ☐

D. Mediation, as it is confidential and no other customers can therefore discover any information about any settlement reached. ☐

E. Litigation, as issuing proceedings is the most likely method to bring the parties to the negotiating table. ☐

Q6 of 90

Flag for review

The defendant is being investigated for a health condition causing them to lose consciousness. One evening after a long day at work, the defendant is driving home when they suddenly feel very unwell. The defendant is only one mile from their home and decides to try and get home where they can rest or call a doctor if they feel worse. The defendant loses consciousness before they reach their destination. With the defendant unconscious, their vehicle mounts the pavement and collides with a couple walking their dog. The couple and dog are seriously injured.

What is the likely outcome regarding the standard of care applied to the defendant?

A. The court will apply the standard of care of a driver suffering impairment and the defendant will not be liable for the accident.

B. The court will apply the standard of care of a reasonable driver and find the defendant should have stopped the car immediately when they felt unwell.

C. The court will apply the standard of care of a professional road user and find the defendant should have steered away from the couple on the pavement.

D. The court will apply the standard of care of a reasonable person and find that it was reasonable for the defendant to continue their journey as they were only one mile away from their home.

E. The court will apply the special standard of care on the basis that the defendant was suffering from an illness and find that the accident was an unavoidable incident that could not have been prevented.

Q7 of 90

Flag for review

A company has four equal shareholders who are also directors. The company adopted the model articles of association as its company constitution, but made some amendments. Three of the director/shareholders would like to remove the fourth director/shareholder as a director as they are not satisfied with her performance in general. The three director/shareholders have given notice of a proposed resolution to remove the fourth director/shareholder from the board, and the board has placed the resolution on the agenda for the next general meeting.

Which of the following statements does not represent an accurate statement of law?

A. The fourth director/shareholder to be removed should receive notice of the proposal to remove.

B. The company's articles of association should be checked for any clause that may give the fourth director/shareholder to be removed weighted voting rights on any resolution to remove.

C. The three director/shareholders cannot use the written resolution procedure to remove the fourth director/shareholder.

D. Any ordinary resolution to remove the fourth director/shareholder will not be effective unless the board gave notice of intention to propose it at least 21 days before the general meeting at which it is proposed.

E. The fourth director/shareholder to be removed is entitled to be heard at the meeting.

Flag for review 🏳

A high street law firm instructs a costs lawyer to advise on litigation costs in an ongoing case.

Which of the following statements best describes the regulatory regime applicable to the costs lawyer?

A. The costs lawyer is subject to the regulation of the Solicitors Regulation Authority and the Costs Lawyer Standards Board. ☐

B. The costs lawyer is subject to the regulation of the Costs Lawyer Standards Board. ☐

C. The costs lawyer is subject to the regulation of the Costs Lawyer Standards Board and is also subject to the Solicitors Regulation Authority whilst providing advice to an authorised law firm. ☐

D. The costs lawyer is not a regulated legal service provider and is not subject to regulation by a regulatory body. ☐

E. The costs lawyer is a regulated legal service provider and is subject to regulation by the Legal Services Board. ☐

Flag for review 🏳

A company has four shareholders who hold shares in the following proportions:
- Shareholder A owns 25%
- Shareholder B owns 33%
- Shareholder C owns 11%
- Shareholder D owns 31%.

Shareholder B is one of the two directors of the company. The other director does not hold any shares in the company. Shareholder C acts as chairperson of the general meetings. The company has unamended model articles as its articles of association.

Which of the following provides the best advice in relation to the company's general meetings?

A. In respect of a shareholders' meeting where all the shareholders are eligible to attend and vote, any of the shareholders can prevent a general meeting being held at short notice. ☐

B. In the event of deadlock on a shareholders' resolution at a shareholders' meeting, Shareholder C, as chairperson, will have a casting vote. ☐

C. In respect of a shareholders' meeting where all shareholders are eligible to attend and vote, Shareholder A will be able to block a special resolution on a poll vote. ☐

D. In order to approve a long-term service contract for Shareholder B, in their capacity as a director, Shareholders A and D would have to vote in favour of the shareholders' resolution as Shareholder B would be unable to vote due to a conflict of interest. ☐

E. In respect of a shareholders' meeting where all the shareholders are eligible to attend and vote, all of the shareholders must agree to call a poll vote at that meeting. ☐

Q10 of 90

Flag for review

The claimant's father worked for many years in factories where asbestos was processed. Each day, the father would return home still in his overalls and give the claimant a hug. Many years later, the claimant developed mesothelioma and brings a claim against one of the factories her father worked in during his 30-year career. The claimant's father worked in three factories and could potentially have been exposed to asbestos at any one of them.

What is the likely outcome of a claim brought by the claimant against one of the factories her father used to work for?

A. The court is likely to find for the claimant on the basis that a claimant suffering from mesothelioma can recover damages from all responsible persons in breach of duty concerning exposure to asbestos.

B. The court is likely to apportion damages to the claimant reflected on the basis of how long her father worked for each factory.

C. The court is likely to reject the claim on the basis that the claimant's condition is too remote from her father's occupation.

D. The court is likely to award damages to the claimant but reduce the amount to reflect contributory negligence on the basis the claimant contributed to her condition by hugging her father each day.

E. The court is likely to only award damages if it considers that there has been a material increase in risk to the claimant to the extent it was foreseeable that she would develop mesothelioma.

Q11 of 90

Flag for review

The owner of a café places an order for a coffee machine through an online website. The owner receives an email from the seller acknowledging receipt of the order and stating that the contract will be concluded on dispatch of the coffee machine. The machine is dispatched two days later.

The owner takes delivery of the machine. Included with the delivery is a document headed 'terms and conditions of sale'. The document contains a term stating that the seller's liability for defective products is limited to £1,000. One week after taking delivery, the coffee machine explodes, causing significant damages to the owner's café. The estimated cost of repair to the café is £10,000.

Which of the following best describes the legal position?

A. As the owner is acting for purposes relating to their business, the seller cannot limit their liability for the defective product.

B. As the owner is of limited bargaining position, it is not reasonable for the seller to limit liability for the defective product.

C. As the owner has been provided with sufficient notice of the term, the term is binding so far as it satisfies the test of reasonableness.

D. As notice of the clause is only provided with the delivery of the machine, the clause is not incorporated into the contract between the owner and the seller.

E. The wording of the clause is not sufficiently clear to cover the relevant basis of liability, as the liability arises in negligence.

Q12 of 90   Flag for review

A solicitor is instructed by a client in a personal injury matter. The limitation period expires four days after the client instructs the solicitor.

Which of the following best explains the steps that should be taken by the solicitor?

A. The solicitor should issue proceedings immediately, thus preserving the limitation period.

B. The solicitor should issue proceedings immediately but request a stay from the court to allow correspondence to be exchanged between the parties that satisfies the terms of the pre-action protocol.

C. The solicitor should write to the opposing party in compliance with the pre-action protocol.

D. The solicitor should write to the opposing party in compliance with the pre-action protocol and apply to the court for an extension of the limitation period.

E. The solicitor should advise the client that proceedings cannot be brought against the defendant as there is insufficient time to comply with the relevant pre-action protocol.

Q13 of 90   Flag for review

A solicitor is representing the defendant employer in a personal injury matter arising from an accident in the workplace. The claimant's case is that he was injured when a forklift truck he was driving crashed into a shelving unit at the defendant's factory. The claimant alleges that he was not properly trained to use the forklift truck. The defendant's case is that the claimant was given adequate training and the accident was caused by his own negligence. The case has been allocated to the multi-track. On the morning of the trial, the defendant produces the training log. It shows that the defendant only gave the claimant a five-minute briefing at the beginning of the day and not the day's training they have previously asserted. The existence of the training log has not been disclosed to the claimant. The solicitor advises that the training log should be disclosed, but the defendant refuses to do so under any circumstances.

Which of the following best describes the approach that the solicitor should take?

A. The solicitor should disclose the training log to the claimant, but not the judge, regardless of the defendant's view.

B. The solicitor should follow the defendant's instructions and make no mention of the training log to the claimant or the judge.

C. The solicitor should disclose the training log to the claimant and the judge, regardless of the defendant's view.

D. The solicitor should withdraw from the case if the defendant continues to refuse disclosure.

E. The solicitor should disclose the training log to the judge, but not the claimant, regardless of the defendant's view.

Q14 of 90   Flag for review 🏳

A large commercial law firm employs a paralegal to assist with a range of administrative tasks. The law firm is regulated by the Solicitors Regulation Authority (SRA). The paralegal has recently completed their law degree but has not completed any other legal qualifications.

Which of the following statements most accurately describes the paralegal's obligations under the SRA Code of Conduct?

A. The paralegal is not subject to the SRA Code of Conduct because they are not a practising solicitor.

B. The paralegal must ensure that they are aware of the contents of the SRA Code of Conduct because they are working for an SRA-regulated law firm. They are not, however, subject to the SRA Code of Conduct.

C. The paralegal must ensure that they are aware of the contents of the SRA Code of Conduct and are subject to the SRA's regulatory regime because they are working for an SRA-regulated law firm.

D. The paralegal is not subject to the SRA Code of Conduct because they are not a qualified solicitor.

E. The paralegal should ensure that they are aware of the contents of the SRA Code of Conduct and will be subject to its regulatory regime if they engage in any reserved activities.

Q15 of 90   Flag for review 🏳

A man places an advertisement in a local newspaper. The advertisement states:
'Digital camera. Bought for £500, but may sell for £100. Contact me at the following address if you wish to buy.'

A woman sees the advertisement and posts a letter saying she will buy the camera for £100, and asks whether it includes a camera case. The man receives the letter and replies, telling the woman that the camera has already been sold. The woman asserts that she has a contract to purchase the camera as she has met the requirements stated in the advertisement.

Which of the following statements best describes the liability of the man?

A. The man has no liability to the woman as the woman was not the first person to accept the man's offer.

B. The man is liable to the woman as the woman accepted the offer, her acceptance being effective as soon as it was posted.

C. The man has no liability to the woman as the advertisement was an invitation to treat and not an offer for sale.

D. The man is liable to the woman as the man did not revoke the offer before the woman's acceptance was effective.

E. The man is not liable to the woman as the woman's letter constituted a counter-offer.

Flag for review

A solicitor is driving their car when they are stopped by the police. The solicitor is breathalysed and is found to be over the drink–drive limit. The solicitor pleads guilty to a charge of driving with excess alcohol and is sentenced by the magistrates' court to a driving ban for 12 months and a fine of £1,000.

Which of the following best describes the solicitor's obligation to the Solicitors Regulation Authority (SRA)?

A. The solicitor must notify the SRA of their conviction within three months' following the date of the conviction. ☐

B. The solicitor is not required to notify the SRA of their conviction as it has nothing to do with their practice as a solicitor. ☐

C. The solicitor is not required to notify the SRA of their conviction as it does not involve any allegation of dishonesty. ☐

D. The solicitor has the discretion to decide whether to notify the SRA of their conviction. ☐

E. The solicitor must notify the SRA of their conviction promptly. ☐

Flag for review

An actor enters into a contract to play the lead role in a film. The production company went to the expense of hiring camera equipment, a director and assistant directors. The actor then withdraws from the production, repudiating the agreement. The production company accepts that this is a breach of contract and brings a claim for damages against the actor.

Which of the following best describes the measure of damage that the court is likely to award?

A Reliance. ☐

B Expectation. ☐

C Wasted expenditure incurred after the breach of contract. ☐

D Loss of opportunity. ☐

E Loss of expected future profit. ☐

Q18 of 90   Flag for review

The police are called to the claimant's home as a neighbour hears shouting. The police arrive, enter into the claimant's house, and find them unresponsive laying on the floor. The police call an ambulance explaining that the claimant is unresponsive and suffering seizures. The ambulance takes over eight minutes to arrive during which time the claimant suffers cardiac arrest and dies. The claimant's family bring a claim against the National Health Service (NHS). The court accepts the medical expert's opinion, which is that, had the paramedics arrived and commenced CPR within an earlier time after the onset of cardiac arrest, the claimant would have had a survival rate of 12%.

What is the likely outcome of a claim for clinical negligence against the NHS?

A. The court is likely to find that liability rests with the police for failing to call an ambulance earlier.

B. The court is likely to find that due to NHS underfunding the failure of the ambulance to attend on time is an inevitable accident.

C. The court will likely accept the medical expert's evidence and find the failure of the paramedics to arrive earlier to have contributed to the claimant's death, and award damages.

D. The court will likely accept the medical expert's evidence but find that the lost chance of survival is not sufficient to base a claim upon.

E. The court will likely award damages but reduce any amount by 88% to reflect contributory negligence.

Q19 of 90   Flag for review

A company enters into a contract with a manufacturer. The manufacturer is to create and supply 100 tee-shirts to the company by 20 May. The contract price is £2,000. The contract states that the company shall pay the full amount once all the tee-shirts are delivered. The contract is frustrated on 10 May. Half of the tee-shirts have been delivered by 10 May. Even after the frustrating event, the company still has buyers for the tee-shirts.

Which of the following statements best describes the effect of frustration on the contract?

A. The company can bring a claim in restitution due to a total failure of consideration.

B. The company will be required to pay the full £2,000 agreed under the contract.

C. The manufacturer will be required to create and supply the remaining tee-shirts under the contract.

D. The court may allow the manufacturer to recover a just sum representing the valuable benefit conferred by their partial performance of the contract.

E. The court may allow the manufacturer to off-set the expenses they incurred in the partial performance of the contract.

Q20 of 90   Flag for review

In a complex claim arising in nuisance, the parties are unable to agree on the principal issues and have reached an impasse. As a result, although disclosure has taken place and the parties have exchanged witness statements, the parties are unwilling to commit to mediation. The parties are willing to consider arbitration, but one party is nervous in case the arbitrator makes a mistake in his judgment.

Which of the following explanations best describes the position if one party felt that the arbitrator had made a mistake?

A. The relevant party can refer the matter back to the arbitrator with an explanation of why they feel the arbitrator has wrongly applied the law. The arbitrator will then reconsider.

B. The relevant party can appeal to the court if they believe that that the arbitrator has wrongly applied the law.

C. The relevant party can seek the permission of the court to challenge the decision of the arbitrator if they believe the arbitrator has wrongly applied the law.

D. The relevant party can request that the matter be heard by a different arbitrator with specific knowledge of the law in the relevant area.

E. The relevant party is bound by the decision and award made by the arbitrator and therefore must comply with its terms.

Q21 of 90   Flag for review

A mid-sized law firm that specialises in personal injury claims has professional indemnity insurance cover of up to £5 million. The firm deals with a wide range of personal injury claims and specialises in high-value-injury claims.

Which of the following statements most accurately describes the extent to which the firm is likely to have fulfilled its obligation to ensure it has adequate and appropriate professional indemnity insurance cover?

A. The firm is likely to have satisfied the requirement that it has adequate and appropriate professional indemnity insurance because the cover exceeds the minimum threshold of £3 million.

B. The firm is likely to have satisfied the requirement that it has adequate and appropriate professional indemnity insurance because the firm is likely to be able to meet any claim liabilities.

C. The firm is likely to have satisfied the requirement that it has adequate and appropriate professional indemnity insurance because the test for establishing whether the cover is sufficient is entirely subjective.

D. The firm is unlikely to have satisfied the requirement that it has adequate and appropriate professional indemnity insurance because the nature of the claims the firm deals with could expose it to substantial claim liabilities that it may not be able to meet.

E. The firm is unlikely to have satisfied the requirement that it has adequate and appropriate professional indemnity insurance because the cover does not meet the appropriate and adequate threshold set out in legislation.

Q22 of 90   Flag for review ⚑

A judge is considering a high-profile appeal case concerning a breach of privacy claim. The claim failed at first instance. The appellant claims that the judge at first instance misinterpreted the meaning of a statutory provision. The case has attracted significant media attention and has been the subject of numerous academic articles. There have also been widespread calls for the law to be reformed. The matter has been discussed in a recent House of Commons debate and the Government has pledged to introduce new legislation that will change the law on privacy.

Which of the following statements most accurately describes the sources the judge may use to interpret the relevant statutory provision?

A. The judge may only refer to the academic literature to assist them in interpreting the relevant statutory provision. ☐

B. The judge may refer to the academic literature and Hansard to assist them in interpreting the relevant provision. ☐

C. The judge may only refer to Hansard to assist them in interpreting the relevant provision. ☐

D. The judge must refer to Hansard to assist them in interpreting the relevant provision because it will ensure the provision is interpreted in accordance with Parliament's wishes. ☐

E. The judge may refer to academic writings to assist them in interpreting the relevant provision if they determine that the relevant statutory provision is unclear or ambiguous. ☐

Q23 of 90   Flag for review ⚑

A man and a woman negotiated for the sale of a business. The negotiations started on 1 January. The woman stated that the business was profitable and that there were no other competitors within a five-mile radius. The man purchased the business in December of the same year. The written contract made no reference to either statement.

Which of the following statements best describes the legal position?

A. The statements made by the woman are likely to be terms of the contract. ☐

B. The statements made by the woman are likely to be representations. ☐

C. The statements made by the woman are likely to be innominate terms. ☐

D. The statements made by the woman cannot be terms of a contract as they were not relied upon by the man. ☐

E. The statements made by the woman cannot be terms of a contract as they were not identified as conditions or warranties. ☐

Q24 of 90   Flag for review

A company needs to raise a substantial sum to finance an acquisition and is negotiating to borrow this amount from a major bank. The company has never given security for any borrowing in the past.

The company's most valuable assets include the machinery in its factory and its stock.

Which of the following security packages for the borrowing is most appropriate?

A. A fixed charge over the machinery and a floating charge over the stock.

B. A fixed charge over both the machinery and the stock.

C. A floating charge over both the machinery and the stock.

D. A fixed charge over the stock and a floating charge over the machinery.

E. A new issue of preference shares to the bank.

Q25 of 90   Flag for review

A man and a woman are equal partners in business. Their friend is going to join the partnership as a new and equal partner.

Which of the following statements does not represent an accurate statement of advice to the man and woman?

A. As the man and woman currently own half of the partnership business each, they will have to surrender approximately 17.5% of the business each so that the friend can own a third of the business as an equal partner.

B. The partnership agreement can be renegotiated so that it can be amended to reflect that there are now three partners.

C. The friend would like to earn interest on their capital injection. There must be a clause included in the new partnership agreement to reflect this as it is not covered by the Partnership Act 1890.

D. Losses can be shared in the same ratios as profits under the partnership agreement.

E. The friend owns a property that the partnership business will use for a small fee. Ownership of the property can be transferred to the partnership business and be owned as a partnership asset.

Q26 of 90   Flag for review 🏳

A solicitor is consulted by a client regarding a personal injury matter. A Belgian resident, driving their own car, negligently crashed into the client in the UK. The client suffered whiplash and a broken clavicle.

Which of the following best describes the advice that the solicitor should give the client concerning the applicable governing law and the appropriate jurisdiction in which proceedings should be issued?

A. The governing law is Belgian law as the car is registered and insured there. The client should issue proceedings in Belgium.

B. The governing law is Belgian law as the defendant is a resident there. The client should issue proceedings in Belgium.

C. The governing law is English law as the client is a resident there. The client should issue proceedings in England and Wales.

D. The governing law is English law as the collision occurred there. The client should issue proceedings in England and Wales.

E. The governing law is English law as the collision occurred there. The client could issue proceedings in either England and Wales or Belgium.

Q27 of 90   Flag for review 🏳

The UK Government has recently enacted legislation that reforms various aspects of youth justice policy.

Which of the following statements most accurately describes the effect of enactment?

A. The legislation will automatically come into effect in Welsh law because the UK Parliament is the sovereign law-making body in respect of all UK law.

B. The legislation will not come into effect in Welsh law unless it is approved by the Welsh Parliament.

C. The legislation will come into effect in Welsh law providing the Welsh Parliament consent to it doing so.

D. The legislation will automatically come into effect in Welsh law because the UK Parliament is the sovereign law-making body in respect of all non-devolved matters.

E. The legislation will not come into effect in Welsh law unless the legislation has been considered and debated by the Welsh Parliament.

Q28 of 90   Flag for review 🏳

A man attends hospital for a routine operation, which is performed by a consultant surgeon. During the operation the anaesthetist fails to monitor the man's oxygen correctly and the man suffers a seizure leading to death. The anaesthetist has been in the post for only two weeks. The man is survived by their civil partner and their civil partner's two children. The man provided financially for their family and the children were treated by the man as their own children.

Who is able to bring a claim for the death of the man?

A   Only the civil partner of the man.

B   The civil partner and the children.

C   Only the children of the civil partner.

D   The eldest child of the civil partner treated as such by the man prior to death.

E   No person may bring a claim as the anaesthetist has a defence due to their inexperience.

Q29 of 90   Flag for review 🏳

The board of directors of a company is trying to gauge the companies' liability to corporation tax.

Which of the following will the board of directors include in its calculation?

A   Distributable profits.

B   Trading income.

C   Profit from the sale of an industrial building.

D   Directors' salaries.

E   Donations to charity.

Q30 of 90   Flag for review 🏳

A woman visits an art gallery salesroom. She sees a painting on the wall and believes it to be the work of a famous artist. She asks the owner of the gallery for the price. The owner, also believing the painting to be the work of a famous artist, states that the price is £20,000. The woman purchases the painting for £20,000.

Two months later, the woman discovers that the painting is not by a famous artist and is only worth approximately £1,000.

Can the woman return the painting for a full refund?

A   Yes, because the painting does not match its description.

B   No, because the owner provided no representation or warranty to the woman that the painting was the work of a famous artist.

C   Yes, because the painting is worth significantly less than the woman believed it to be.

D   No, because rescission of the contract is not possible due to a lapse of time.

E   Yes, because the owner of the painting misrepresented the price to the woman.

Q31 of 90   Flag for review 🏳

Three friends are setting up a new company and have sought advice regarding the formalities necessary to set up the new company.

Which of the following must be filed at Companies House when forming a new company?

A.   Articles of association.

B.   Memorandum of association.

C.   Form AD01 (change the registered office).

D.   Form IN01 (incorporation).

E.   Form AP01 (appointment of director).

Q32 of 90   Flag for review 🏳

A company is struggling to pay all of its debts as they fall due. One of the company's major creditors issues a statutory demand requiring the company to pay the money that it owes within 21 days. The company pays this major creditor but insolvency proceedings are brought and an administrator is appointed six weeks later. The administrator will assess all of the business of the company so that the best interests of the company and all of its creditors will be assessed. The administrator will examine all recent transactions in order to assess whether there should be applications to have any of them set aside.

Which of the following best describes the likely position of the administrator regarding this payment?

A.   The administrator can immediately seek to have the payment set aside on the grounds that the company was insolvent at the time of the payment.

B.   The administrator is unlikely to seek to have the payment set aside as the payment was made under a real threat of insolvency proceedings being brought against the company.

C.   The administrator can immediately seek to have the payment set aside on the grounds that this payment would be a preference.

D.   The administrator can immediately seek to have the payment set aside on the grounds that this payment would amount to a transaction defrauding creditors.

E.   The administrator is unlikely to seek to have the payment set aside as the payment was made in the normal course of business and the company acted in good faith.

Q35 of 90

The clients wish to set up a new business together but do not know whether they would like to trade as a partnership, limited liability partnership (LLP) or company. The business will buy raw materials, produce goods and sell to other businesses. The clients would like to attract business from multinational customers. They are likely to need to take out substantial loans in the future to expand but wish to retain control themselves. They are likely to be taking on employees.

Which of the following best describes the type of business that the clients should set up and the correct justification for it?

A. The clients should be advised that a company is the best type of business for their needs. This is because the shareholders' liability for debts would be limited, they would be able to attract finance because companies can grant floating charges and the company is a widely recognised business medium worldwide.

B. The clients should be advised that an LLP is the best type of business for their needs. This is because the partners' liability for debts would be limited, they would be able to attract finance because LLPs can grant floating charges and the LLP is a widely recognised business medium worldwide.

C. The clients should be advised that a partnership is the best type of business for their needs. This is because the process is informal and there is no obvious reason why the clients would need their liability for the business's debts to be limited, and they would be able to secure any future borrowing by way of a fixed charge.

D. The clients should be advised that either an LLP or a partnership is the best type of business for their needs. This is because there will only be two partners, and there is no need to start a company and have the burden of the legal and administrative requirements it brings.

E. The clients should be advised that either a company or an LLP is the best type of business for their needs. This is because either business type will enable them to run the business in a more organised way, whereas partnerships tend to be run more informally because no partnership agreement is necessary.

Q34 of 90

A solicitor acts for a client in relation to a property transaction. On the day the transaction is due to complete, the solicitor becomes aware of information that causes them to suspect their client will be using the transaction to launder money.

Which of the following statements most accurately describes the solicitor's obligations under anti-money laundering regulations?

A. The solicitor must report their concerns to the nominated officer who should then make a suspicious activity report to the relevant authority.

B. The solicitor should proceed with the transaction and should make a disclosure to the nominated officer as soon as practicable.

C. The solicitor should proceed with the transaction as there is no firm evidence that the transaction will be used to launder proceeds of crime.

D. The solicitor should inform the client of their concerns in order to establish whether the transaction is likely to be used for money laundering purposes.

E. The solicitor should report their concerns to the nominated officer and then promptly inform the client that a report has been made.

Q35 of 90   Flag for review

A client would like to set up their own business, which they will run as a sole trader. The client would like to work alone but they need to raise funds to start and run the business.

Which of the following statements describes the best option available to the client in this situation?

A.   The client could issue shares in their business.

B.   The client could act as a guarantor on a loan by their bank to a third party.

C.   The client could issue bonds or securities in order to raise funds.

D.   The client could take a loan from a bank in return for a floating charge over all their assets.

E.   The client could borrow money from a third party.

Q36 of 90   Flag for review

A client instructed a solicitor in relation to damage that they have recently discovered to their property. Sixteen years ago, the client instructed a company to knock through two walls to create an open-plan kitchen, dining room and living room. Eight months ago, whilst carrying out redecoration work, the client discovered significant structural damage to their property which will cost in the region of £150,000 to rectify. An expert confirmed last week that the structural damage has been caused by the company failing to deal with the removal of a supporting wall properly.

Which of the following best represents how the solicitor should advise the client regarding limitation?

A.   The company is in breach of contract. The limitation period is six years following the date of the breach. The limitation period has expired, and the client will need to apply to the court to extend the limitation period to enable proceedings to be issued.

B.   The company has been negligent. The limitation period is three years from the date on which the damage occurred. The limitation period has expired, and the client will need to apply to the court to extend the limitation period to enable proceedings to be issued.

C.   The company has been negligent. The limitation period is six years from the date on which the damage occurred. The limitation period has expired, and the client will need to apply to the court to extend the limitation period to enable proceedings to be issued.

D.   The company has been negligent. The limitation period is three years from the date on which the client first knew about the cause of action. The client discovered the damage eight months ago and can therefore issue proceedings.

E.   The company has been negligent. The limitation period is three years from the date on which the client first knew about the cause of action. However, due to the time which has elapsed since the negligent act or omission occurred, the client will be statute barred from bringing a claim.

Q37 of 90   Flag for review 🏳

The UK Prime Minister has recently been the subject of a number of scandals and is very unpopular with the public. Despite this, a recent vote of confidence confirms that the Prime Minister still enjoys the support of the majority of the House of Commons. The Prime Minister has publicly stated that they will not resign from their position. Members of the public have therefore set up an online campaign requesting that the King dismisses the Prime Minister from office.

Which of the following statements most accurately describes the King's power to dismiss the Prime Minister?

A. As Head of State, the King has the power to dismiss the Prime Minister if he feels it is appropriate to do so.

B. Under the Royal Prerogative, the King appoints the Prime Minister and may, therefore, dismiss him from office if he wishes to do so.

C. As Head of State, the King appoints the Prime Minister and may, therefore, dismiss him from office if he wishes to do so.

D. Under the Royal Prerogative, the King appoints the Prime Minister and may, therefore, dismiss him from office if he wishes to do so. However, by convention the Prime Minister will remain in office providing he maintains the support of the majority of the House of Commons.

E. Although the King is Head of State, because of the separation of powers the King has no powers to appoint or dismiss the Prime Minister from office.

Q38 of 90   Flag for review 🏳

A client is a partner in a partnership. Due to the economic downturn, the latest projections indicate that there is a risk that the business may become insolvent and the client is concerned about their potential liability should insolvency proceedings follow.

Which of the following statements best describes the potential liability of the client should the partnership become insolvent?

A. The client could be liable to the extent of their original investment in the partnership.

B. The client could be equally liable for all the debts of the partnership.

C. The client could be jointly and severally liable for all the debts of the partnership.

D. The client could be jointly liable for all the debts of the partnership.

E. The client could be liable for the debts of the partnership to the extent agreed in the partnership agreement as to loss-sharing.

Q39 of 90   Flag for review 🏳

A client consults a solicitor in connection with a claim for damages of £60,000 arising from a personal injury flowing from a road traffic accident. The client argues that the opponent caused the collision because they swerved into the client's vehicle, causing it to change course and strike a tree. The opponent denies liability on the basis that an inspection of the client's vehicle revealed a fault with the steering causing it to lock, breaking the chain of causation. The client's losses are also contested as they are self-employed. Forensic accountants have been instructed for both parties, who have disagreed on their assessment of the value of the loss of future earnings the client is claiming.

Which of the following best represents the court in which the claim should be commenced, and why?

A. The claim should be commenced in the High Court as the value is over £50,000 and the facts are complex. ☐

B. The claim should be commenced in the High Court despite the value of the claim being under £100,000 as the facts are complex. ☐

C. The claim should be commenced in the County Court despite the value being over £50,000 as the facts are not sufficiently complex to warrant issuing in the High Court. ☐

D. The claim should be commenced in the County Court as the value of the claim is under £100,000 and the facts are not sufficiently complex to warrant issuing in the High Court. ☐

E. The claim should be commenced in the County Court as, despite the complex facts, the value of the claim is under £100,000. ☐

Q40 of 90   Flag for review 🏳

A solicitor has recently completed a high-value property transaction on behalf of a new client. It has now come to light that the transaction was used for money laundering purposes. The solicitor was reluctant to proceed with the transaction because they were concerned it may be used for money laundering purposes. The solicitor promptly informed the firm's nominated officer of their concerns. The nominated officer stated that they would investigate the matter in due course. A Suspicious Activity Report was not submitted to the National Crime Agency (NCA).

Which of the following statements most accurately outlines the solicitor's position in respect of liability under the Proceeds of Crime Act (POCA) 2002?

A. The solicitor will most likely be liable for the offence of failing to make a disclosure. ☐

B. The solicitor has not committed a failure to make a Suspicious Activity Report offence under the POCA 2002 because it is the duty of the nominated officer to make such reports to the NCA. ☐

C. The solicitor will most likely be liable for failing to make a Suspicious Activity Report. ☐

D. The solicitor will not be liable for an offence under the POCA 2002 because they had no actual knowledge or proof of money laundering. ☐

E. The solicitor is likely to have fulfilled their obligation to make a Suspicious Activity Report by disclosing their concerns to the firm's nominated officer. ☐

Flag for review

A solicitor is advising a client in respect of a number of matters relating to their farming business. The solicitor advises the client that a piece of European Union (EU) law which is still in force requires their business to comply with a number of animal welfare regulations. The EU law in question was in effect on 31 January 2020 and is still in force.

Which of the following statements most accurately describes the legislation in question?

A. The legislation would be classified as retained EU law because it was part of the body of EU law that applied on the day that the UK ceased to be a member of the EU.

B. The legislation would be classified as retained EU law because it has not been repealed by the Withdrawal Agreement.

C. The legislation would be classified as retained EU law because it is defined as such by the Court of Justice of the European Union.

D. The legislation would be classified as retained EU law because it was in effect at the time the Withdrawal Agreement was ratified by the UK Parliament.

E. The legislation would be classified as retained EU law because it was part of the body of EU law that applied until the implementation period completion date.

Flag for review

A man enters a car dealership and negotiates for the purchase of a new car. The man completes and signs a sales agreement in the name of 'Mr Smith'. The man is not Mr Smith and is purchasing the car fraudulently. The man drives the car away the same day. The man then sells the car to a woman. One week later, the dealership discovers that the man is not Mr Smith, and they bring a claim against the woman to recover the car.

Can the car dealership recover the car from the woman?

A. No, as the contract between the dealership and the man was enforceable.

B. Yes, as the contract for the sale of the car is voidable.

C. No, as the woman, a third party, has acquired rights in the car.

D. Yes, as the contract for the sale of the car is void for mistake as to identity.

E. No, as the contract between the man and the woman was the result of fraud.

Q43 of 90   Flag for review 🏳

A trainee solicitor works in a small high-street law firm. Recently, the solicitor became aware that another trainee solicitor at the firm may have accidentally committed a minor breach of confidentiality whilst working on a client's file. The solicitor reports their concerns to one of the partners in the firm and questions what actions, if any, they must take with the Solicitors Regulation Authority (SRA).

Which of the following statements most accurately describes the solicitor's actions?

A. The solicitor has discharged their reporting obligations under the SRA Code of Conduct because the solicitor has reported the potential breach to a senior member of staff.

B. The solicitor has failed to discharge their reporting obligations under the SRA Code of Conduct as the SRA must be informed of all potential breaches of confidentiality.

C. The solicitor has failed to discharge their reporting obligations under the SRA Code of Conduct as the firm's Compliance Officer for Legal Practice must be informed of all potential breaches of confidentiality.

D. The solicitor is not bound by any reporting obligations under the SRA Code of Conduct because the solicitor is not yet fully qualified.

E. The solicitor has discharged their reporting obligations under the SRA Code of Conduct because they have reported the potential breach to a senior member of staff. The senior solicitor is responsible for reporting the issue to the firm's Compliance Officer for Legal Practice.

Q44 of 90   Flag for review 🏳

A solicitor becomes aware that a paralegal within the firm has been the subject of harassment by a senior partner. The senior partner continually telephones her on her mobile phone and at home, and sends her inappropriate messages, texts and e-mails. The paralegal has not reported the matter to anyone else. The solicitor is concerned about the effect this behaviour is having on the paralegal and their responsibilities under the Solicitors Regulation Authority (SRA) Code of Conduct.

Which of the following best reflects what the solicitor should do in the circumstances?

A. The solicitor must report the alleged harassment to the firm's Compliance Officer for Legal Practice.

B. The solicitor must notify the SRA of the alleged harassment.

C. The solicitor must notify the SRA of the alleged harassment and may inform the firm's Compliance Officer for Legal Practice.

D. The solicitor should take no action in respect of the alleged harassment.

E. The solicitor should confront the senior partner directly and challenge him on the alleged harassment.

Q45 of 90   Flag for review 🏳

A company entered into a contract with a supplier for the delivery of a drinks bottling machine at a price of £100,000. The company is to use the machine as part of its everyday business manufacturing soft drinks. Unknown to the supplier, the company also intends to use the machine to satisfy a lucrative contract with a vineyard that is experimenting by using the machine for an unusual and state-of-the-art bottling technique.

The contract contains a clause that the supplier shall pay the company £10,000 for every week that the machine is delivered late. The supplier delivers the machine two weeks late. As result, the company suffers a loss of £2,000 from its soft drink business. The company also suffers a loss of £10,000 as it is unable to perform the contract with the vineyard.

Solicitors acting on behalf of the company bring a claim of £20,000 in damages against the supplier.

Which of the following best describes the amount the court is likely to award the company?

A. £20,000. ☐

B. £12,000. ☐

C. £10,000. ☐

D. £8,000. ☐

E. £2,000. ☐

Q46 of 90   Flag for review 🏳

Improvement works are taking place on a busy motorway. A contractor working on the improvement works drives their lorry into the barriers separating the traffic and, as a result, the motorway is closed for repair. Motorists are stranded on the motorway for five hours. One woman is travelling on the motorway to a job interview and fails to arrive. The woman is not offered another opportunity and the company appoint another candidate.

Is the woman able to bring a claim against the contractor who drove the lorry for her loss of salary caused by failing to be appointed at the job interview?

A Yes, the woman has suffered consequential loss caused by the contractor's negligence. ☐

B No, the contractor has caused economic loss by damaging property of a third party. ☐

C Yes, the woman has suffered economic loss caused by damage to property of a third party. ☐

D No, as although the woman has suffered consequential loss her damage is too remote. ☐

E Yes, the contractor owed the woman a duty of care not to cause her economic loss. ☐

Q47 of 90   Flag for review 🏴

A claim form is issued by the court on Monday 14 September and sent to the claimant to effect service personally. The claimant posts the claim form through the letterbox of the correct address of the defendant at 3.35pm on Friday 18 September.

Which of the following best reflects the correct date of deemed service?

A.   The claim form is deemed served on Friday 18 September.

B.   The claim form is deemed served on Saturday 19 September.

C.   The claim form is deemed served on Sunday 20 September.

D.   The claim form is deemed served on Monday 21 September.

E.   The claim form is deemed served on Tuesday 22 September.

Q48 of 90   Flag for review 🏴

A woman bought a new car from a professional car dealer. The next day the car would not start. This was due to a serious defect within the engine. The woman returned the car to the dealer and demanded a full refund. The dealer refused to refund the woman and instead only offered to repair the car.

Does the woman have to accept the offer of repair?

A.   No, because the car is not of satisfactory quality.

B.   Yes, as the offer of repair is reasonable in the circumstances.

C.   No, because the car does not match its description.

D.   Yes, as the defect was discovered shortly after the purchase.

E.   No, because the car is not fit for purpose.

Q49 of 90   Flag for review 🏴

A newly qualified legal executive has recently taken up a position in a law firm. The firm is classified as a legal service provider and is subject to regulation by the Solicitors Regulation Authority (SRA). A solicitor within the firm asks her to carry on some reserved legal activities under his supervision. The solicitor is authorised to carry on reserved legal activities himself but is unable to manage his hectic workload without some additional assistance.

Which of the following statements most accurately describes the regulatory position with regards to reserved legal activities?

A. The legal executive may carry on reserved legal activities because she is employed by, and will work under the supervision of, a person who is authorised to carry on those reserved legal activities.

B. The legal executive may not carry on reserved legal activities because chartered legal executives are not classified as legal service providers and may not therefore carry on reserved legal activities.

C. The legal executive may carry on reserved legal activities because chartered legal executives are classified as legal service providers and may carry on all reserved legal activities.

D. The legal executive may carry on reserved legal activities provided they are registered with, and regulated by, the SRA.

E. The legal executive may not carry on any reserved legal activities as she has not gained practice rights to carry on reserved legal activities herself.

Q50 of 90   Flag for review 🏴

A solicitor wishes to appear in court on behalf of their client in a criminal matter. The case will be considered by the magistrates' court.

Which of the following best describes the solicitor's rights of audience in this matter?

A. The solicitor can appear in the magistrates' court on behalf of their client as solicitors are automatically granted rights of audience when they are admitted to the roll of solicitors.

B. The solicitor can appear in the magistrates' court on behalf of their client if they have undertaken the relevant assessments in criminal advocacy and have successfully applied for higher rights of audience.

C. The solicitor can appear in the magistrates' court on behalf of their client if they have permission from the court.

D. The solicitor can appear in the magistrates' court on behalf of their client if they have undertaken the relevant assessments in criminal advocacy and have successfully applied for rights of audience.

E. The solicitor can appear in the magistrates' court on behalf of their client if they have undertaken the relevant assessments in criminal advocacy.

Q51 of 90   Flag for review

In the course of a trial, there is a dispute between the parties as to whether an exclusion clause in a contract protects the defendant in a claim for breach of contract.

What rule of construction is the court likely to apply to resolve this dispute?

A. The court will interpret any ambiguity in favour of the party wishing to rely on the clause.

B. The court will interpret the clause based on what a reasonable person would have intended in the circumstances.

C. The court will interpret any ambiguity in the clause strictly against the party wishing to rely on the clause.

D. The court will interpret the clause so as to give effect to the intentions of the parties.

E. The court will interpret the clause so as to avoid an absurd result.

Q52 of 90   Flag for review

A solicitor becomes aware of a serious breach of the Solicitors Regulation Authority (SRA) Code of Conduct by their firm.

Which of the following best reflects the obligation of a solicitor when faced with a breach of the SRA Code of Conduct?

A. A solicitor must report to the SRA any facts or matters that they reasonably believe are capable of amounting to a serious breach of their regulatory arrangements by any person regulated by the SRA promptly.

B. A solicitor must report to their client any misconduct or other reprehensible behaviour by any person regulated by the SRA promptly.

C. A solicitor must only report criminal offences by any person regulated by the SRA promptly.

D. A solicitor must report to their client any facts or matters that they reasonably believe are capable of amounting to a serious breach of their regulatory arrangements by any person regulated by the SRA promptly.

E. A solicitor must report to the SRA any misconduct or other reprehensible behaviour by any person regulated by the SRA promptly.

Q53 of 90   Flag for review 🏳

The claimant suffers an accident at work whilst lifting heavy boxes onto pallets in the warehouse. The claimant brings a claim against their employer on the basis that they had failed to offer any manual handling training. The employer admits liability but disputes the value of the claim. Medical evidence shows that the claimant suffered a ruptured disc in their spine as a result of the accident. The claimant had suffered a back injury in a skiing accident in their youth which had left them with a pre-existing issue with their back. The employer argues that the spinal injury suffered in the accident at work would not have been so serious had the claimant not had a pre-existing issue and they wish to reduce the claimant's damages to reflect this.

Which of the following best reflects the court's likely view of the employer's argument?

A. The court will likely accept that the claimant has a pre-existing injury and reduce the claimant's damages to reflect this. ☐

B. The court will likely find that the employer has a complete defence to the claim. ☐

C. The court will likely find that the pre-existing injury breaks the chain of causation. ☐

D. The court will likely find that but for the pre-existing injury, the claimant would not have suffered further injury. ☐

E. The court will likely take the claimant as they find them and not reduce the claimant's damages. ☐

Q54 of 90   Flag for review 🏳

A partner of a large commercial law firm becomes aware that the expiry date for the firm's professional indemnity insurance has just passed. The firm has not renewed the policy, put an alternative policy in place or notified the Solicitors Regulation Authority (SRA) that the policy has elapsed. The expiry date for the policy was four days ago.

Which of the following statements most accurately sets out the status of the firm's professional indemnity insurance cover?

A. The firm does not have any professional indemnity insurance because the policy expired four days ago. ☐

B. The firm does not have any professional indemnity insurance in place and must cease acting for all clients until an adequate and appropriate indemnity insurance policy is in effect. ☐

C. The firm does not have valid professional indemnity insurance because the policy has elapsed and the firm has not informed the SRA. ☐

D. The firm has entered an Extended Policy Period and may continue to act on behalf of its clients for the next 30 days. ☐

E. The firm has entered an Extended Policy Period and may continue to act on behalf of its clients for up to 30 days from the expiry date. The firm must notify the SRA within five working days of the firm entering the Extended Policy Period. ☐

Q55 of 90   Flag for review 🏷

A claimant has brought a claim in the County Court against their neighbour for recovery of a sum of money loaned by them to the neighbour. The neighbour has neither acknowledged service nor filed a defence. The claim form and particulars of the claim were deemed served 17 days ago.

Which of the following best describes the advice the claimant's solicitor should give their client about obtaining judgment in default?

A. The claimant may obtain default judgment of an acknowledgment of service or a defence being filed by filing a request in the relevant practice form and an accompanying fee. ☐

B. The claimant may obtain default judgment by filing a request in the relevant practice form after 28 days from the deemed date of service. ☐

C. The claimant may obtain default judgment of an acknowledgement of service or a defence being filed by sending a letter to the court requesting such a judgment be made, with an accompanying fee. ☐

D. The claimant may not obtain default judgment in the County Court as the County Court has no jurisdiction to deal with the remedy sought. ☐

E. The claimant may not obtain default judgment in this claim as it falls within a category in which a default judgment cannot be obtained. ☐

Q56 of 90   Flag for review 🏷

A solicitor defends a woman in a personal injury dispute. The woman's gross income is £2,000 per month, her disposable income is £800 per month, and her disposable capital is £6,000. The woman seeks legal aid in the form of legal representation. The solicitor is satisfied that the woman passes the merits test, but is unsure as to whether the woman passes the means test.

Which of the following best describes whether the woman is likely to succeed in her application for civil legal aid?

A. The woman does not qualify for civil legal aid because her gross income is over the prescribed limit. ☐

B. The woman does not qualify for civil legal aid because both her gross income and her disposable capital are over the prescribed limit. ☐

C. The woman does not qualify for civil legal aid because her disposable income is over the prescribed limit. ☐

D. The woman does not qualify for civil legal aid because both her disposable income and her disposable capital are over the prescribed limit. ☐

E. The woman does not qualify for civil legal aid because her disposable capital is over the prescribed limit. ☐

Q57 of 90   Flag for review

A company is served with proceedings. The date of service coincides with a high volume of mail and, as a result, the envelope enclosing the proceedings is accidently shredded before it is opened. A further letter from the court is received by the company enclosing an order awarding judgment in default in favour of the claimant on the basis of the company's failure to acknowledge service of the original claim form by the relevant deadline.

Which of the following best represents the course of action the company should take?

A. The company can apply to set aside judgment in default on the discretionary ground, provided it can show that it has a reasonable prospect of successfully defending the claim and there is a good reason why it did not respond, provided this is done promptly.

B. The company can apply to set aside judgment in default on the mandatory ground, provided this is done promptly.

C. The company can apply to set aside judgment in default on the discretionary ground. The only way of doing so is to show that it has a reasonable prospect of successfully defending the claim.

D. The company can apply to set aside judgment in default on the discretionary ground. The only way of doing this is to show that there is a good reason why it did not respond.

E. The company can apply to set aside judgment in default on the discretionary ground, provided it can show that it has a reasonable prospect of successfully defending the claim or there is a good reason why it did not respond, provided this is done promptly.

Q58 of 90   Flag for review

The claimant is walking home from work one day when they witness an explosion on a residential street. A defective gas pipe at a property had fractured, causing a leak that ignited when one of the residents turned on their oven. Several houses are destroyed and many of the residents are seriously injured or killed. The claimant was walking directly outside the property that exploded but was not physically injured. They call the emergency services and try to help rescuers who arrive on the scene. When the claimant arrives home, they have a physical reaction to what they have witnessed and start to vomit. The claimant is unable to sleep for weeks and eventually attends their doctor where they are diagnosed with post-traumatic stress disorder (PTSD).

Is the claimant able to bring a claim in negligence in respect of the diagnosed PTSD?

A. Yes, on the basis that the claimant has suffered injury as a secondary victim.

B. No, on the basis that the claimant is not sufficiently proximate to the zone of physical danger.

C. Yes, on the basis that the claimant has suffered physical injury as a primary victim.

D. No, on the basis that the claimant has no tie of love and affection with the occupants of the properties.

E. Yes, on the basis that the claimant has suffered psychiatric injury as a primary victim.

Q59 of 90   Flag for review

The claimant in a civil case intends to appeal the High Court's decision. The case, which concerns a low-value contract law dispute, was initially considered by a High Court judge. The claimant wishes to appeal on the basis of a point of law of general public importance. The decision is unlikely to be of particular significance and does not raise issues of national importance. The claimant would like the issue to be resolved as quickly as possible because they are experiencing serious health issues.

Which of the following statements most accurately explains the correct route of appeal?

A. The appeal would most likely be heard by the Court of Appeal (Civil Division). The leapfrog procedure is unlikely to be applicable because the case concerns a relatively low-value civil claim.

B. The appeal would most likely be heard by the Supreme Court. The leapfrog procedure is likely to be applicable because the case involves a point of law of general public importance.

C. The appeal would most likely be heard by the Court of Appeal (Civil Division) because the Supreme Court does not have the jurisdiction to consider appeals from the High Court.

D. The appeal would most likely be heard by the Court of Appeal (Civil Division) because it is unlikely that the benefits of early consideration by the Supreme Court outweigh the benefits of consideration by the Court of Appeal.

E. The appeal is most likely to be heard by the Supreme Court. The leapfrog procedure may be used to expedite appeal cases concerning points of law of general public importance where there is a good reason to refer the appeal directly to the Supreme Court. In this case, the fact that the claimant is suffering serious health issues would likely constitute a good reason for using the leapfrog procedure.

Q60 of 90   Flag for review

A number of national newspapers have reported that a high-profile and wealthy businessman has been involved in a widespread sexual harassment scandal. The reports claim that the businessman kissed and touched female members of staff without their consent. The businessman used his substantial wealth and influence to encourage the female members of staff to sign non-disclosure agreements to prohibit them from discussing any details of the claims. The businessman also successfully applied for an injunction to prevent the newspaper identifying him as the alleged perpetrator. Concerned by the reports, a member of the House of Lords discloses the identity of the businessman during the course of parliamentary debates.

Which of the following statements best describes the effect of parliamentary privilege in this case?

A. The disclosure of identity would be protected by parliamentary privilege.

B. The disclosure of identity would be liable for breaching the injunction.

C. The disclosure of identity would not be covered by parliamentary privilege.

D. The disclosure of identity would not be covered by parliamentary privilege because an injunction was in place to prevent such a disclosure being made.

E. The disclosure of identity would not be covered by parliamentary privilege because the reports have not been subject to any form of criminal investigation.

G51 of 90   Flag for review 🏴

A group of former solicitors are setting up a will-writing business. The business will only offer will-drafting services and will not engage in any reserved legal activities. The business intends to charge clients for their services.

Which of the following statements most accurately describes the level of professional indemnity insurance (PII) cover the business will need, as required by the Solicitors Regulation Authority (SRA)?

A. The SRA will require the business to have PII cover of up to £3 million for any one claim. ☐

B. The SRA will require the business to have PII cover that is adequate. ☐

C. The SRA will require the business to have PII cover that is appropriate. ☐

D. The SRA will not require the business to have any PII insurance cover. ☐

E. The SRA will require the business to have PII cover that is both adequate and appropriate. ☐

G52 of 90   Flag for review 🏴

A solicitor has been approached by a new client who wishes to engage their services in a high-profile and complex contractual negotiation. The solicitor s being asked to draft the proposed terms of a contract should the new client be awarded the contract. During the initial consultation, the solicitor discovers that they have already been retained by another client in the same matter. The current client retained the solicitor on the specific instruction that the solicitor could not act for any other party interested in the award of the particular contract. The new client is offering to pay the solicitor a higher price than the current client.

Which of the following best describes what the solicitor can do in accordance with the Solicitors Regulation Authority (SRA) Code of Conduct?

A. The solicitor can act for both the new client and the current client without disclosing the potential conflict of interest. ☐

B. The solicitor cannot act for the new client as there is a conflict of interest between the new client and the current client. ☐

C. The solicitor can cease to act for the current client, and act for the new client on the basis that the new client is offering a higher price for the solicitor's services. ☐

D. The solicitor cannot act for the new client as there is an own interest conflict. ☐

E. The solicitor can act for both the new client and the current client but must disclose the potential conflict of interest. ☐

Q63 of 90   Flag for review 🏳

An employer took out a group insurance policy. The policy named the employer as the 'insured' and a number of employees as 'insured persons'. The employees pay an annual fee to the employer for the policy. One of the employees was injured on the employer's premises. The insurer pays the employer a sum of money under the policy.

Is the employee entitled to recover the sum from the employer that was paid by the insurer?

A. Yes, because the employee provided valid consideration to the employer.

B. No, because the contract is between the employer and the insurer only.

C. Yes, because there is a presumption that the employee is intended to have a right of enforceability.

D. No, because no consideration moves from the employee to the insurer.

E. No, because the employer has discretion as to whether to pass the payment to the employee.

Q64 of 90   Flag for review 🏳

A claimant issues proceedings against a defendant for breach of implied terms. The claim form and the particulars of claim are served on the defendant by the court. The defendant intends to defend the proceedings and also to make a counterclaim, but it will take some time to gather the relevant information for both the defence and counterclaim.

Which of the following best describes how the defendant should proceed?

A. The defendant should file an acknowledgement of service, defence and counterclaim within 28 days after service of the claim form and particulars of claim.

B. The defendant should file an acknowledgement of service within seven days after service of the claim form and particulars of claim, and a defence and counterclaim within 21 days of the acknowledgement of service.

C. The defendant should file an acknowledgement of service within 14 days after service of the claim form and particulars of claim, and a defence and counterclaim within 28 days after service of the claim form and particulars of claim.

D. The defendant should file an acknowledgement of service within 14 days after service of the claim form and particulars of claim, and a defence and counterclaim within 14 days of the acknowledgement of service.

E. The defendant should file an acknowledgement of service within 14 days after service of the claim form and particulars of claim, and a defence and counterclaim within 28 days of the acknowledgement of service.

Flag for review

A newly qualified solicitor is retained by a client in a business dispute between the client and a competitor. The solicitor has a personal relationship with an employee of the competitor.

Which of the following is the most relevant Principle of the Solicitors Regulation Authority (SRA) Code of Conduct to the conduct of the solicitor?

A. The solicitor must act in a way that upholds the constitutional principle of the rule of law, and the proper administration of justice.

B. The solicitor must act in a way that encourages equality, diversity and inclusion.

C. The solicitor must act in a way that upholds public trust and confidence in the solicitors' profession and in legal services provided by authorised persons.

D. The solicitor must act with integrity.

E. The solicitor must act with independence.

Flag for review

A client has a taxable income of £70,000 which includes dividend income of £20,000.

Which of the following statements best describes the treatment of the client's dividend income?

A. The entire amount of dividend income will be taxed at the basic rate of income tax as the amount of dividend income falls below the current basic rate threshold.

B. The entire amount of the client's dividend income will be taxed at the higher rate of income tax as it will all come within the higher rate band.

C. The first £2,000 of the client's dividend income will be taxed at 0% and the remainder at the basic rate of income tax.

D. The first £2,000 of the client's dividend income will be taxed at 0% and the remainder at the higher rate of income tax.

E. As the dividend income comes from shares in a trading company, the income is exempt from income tax and will be subject to corporation tax.

Flag for review

A solicitor is dealing with a matter that is being considered by a High Court judge.

Which of the following statements most accurately describes the jurisdiction of High Court judges?

A. High Court judges may only consider cases before the High Court.

B. High Court judges may only consider cases before the High Court, the Crown Court and the Family Court.

C. High Court judges may only consider cases before the High Court and the Family Court.

D. High Court judges may only consider cases before the High Court and the Crown Court.

E. High Court judges may only consider cases before the High Court and the County Court.

Q68 of 90   Flag for review 🏳

A defendant is served with a claim form and particulars of claim. The defendant wishes to defend the claim. Five years ago, the defendant loaned the claimant a sum of money to be repaid in 36 monthly instalments commencing on the date the loan money was advanced.

Which of the following reflects the best way the defendant can proceed?

A. The defendant should file a counterclaim against the claimant at the same time as the defence is filed. It does not matter that the facts are unconnected to the original claim; the defendant is entitled to commence a counterclaim. ☐

B. The defendant should file a separate claim against the claimant immediately. As the facts are unconnected to the original claim it cannot be dealt with by way of counterclaim, but the defendant is entitled to issue proceedings against the claimant separately. ☐

C. The defendant should seek the court's permission to bring a separate claim against the claimant immediately. As the facts are unconnected to the original claim it cannot be dealt with by way of counterclaim, but the defendant is entitled to issue proceedings against the claimant separately with permission of the court. ☐

D. The defendant should wait until the current proceedings are concluded and then issue a claim against the claimant separately. As the facts are unconnected to the original claim it cannot be dealt with by way of counterclaim, but the defendant is entitled to issue proceedings against the claimant separately. ☐

E. The defendant should apply for the permission of the court to file a counterclaim against the claimant immediately. It does not matter that the facts are unconnected to the original claim, the defendant is entitled to commence a counterclaim, but the defendant will need permission from the court to do so. ☐

Q69 of 90   Flag for review

A lender entered into a loan agreement with a business. The loan was for £120,000 and was to be repaid in 12 equal instalments of £10,000. The business paid the first 11 instalments as they fell due. Shortly before the final instalment was due, the lender approached the business and promised that they would accept £5,000 for the final instalment. In exchange for the lender's promise, the business would provide free staff training to the lender's employees. The business paid £5,000 for the final instalment and provided the staff training as agreed.

Two months later, the business received a letter from the lender's solicitors demanding that the business pays the outstanding £5,000, plus the interest accrued on the debt.

Which of the following statements best describes the liability of the business to pay the amount claimed?

A. The business is not liable to pay the amount claimed as their payment of £115,000 under the agreement will constitute a practical benefit to the lender.

B. The business is liable to pay the amount claimed as the staff training was free and had no economic value.

C. The business is not liable to pay the amount claimed as the business can rely upon the doctrine of promissory estoppel.

D. The business is liable to pay the amount claimed as part-payment of a debt is not good consideration.

E. The business is not liable to pay the amount claimed as the provision of the staff development is sufficient consideration to bind the lender to the promise to accept a lesser amount.

Q70 of 90   Flag for review

A small law firm has recently advertised a position for a full-time civil litigation solicitor. The deadline for applications has now passed. The three managing partners of the firm agree to 'sift' the applications by removing all applications from women who are aged 25 to 35. They all agree that women in this age group are likely to need substantial time off from work for maternity-related reasons so it would be preferable to remove such candidates from the pool of applicants before invitations for interviews are sent out.

Which of the following statements most accurately describes the actions of the partners?

A. The actions of the partners amount to victimisation under the Equality Act 2010.

B. The actions of the partners amount to indirect discrimination under the Equality Act 2010.

C. The actions of the partners would not constitute prohibited conduct under the Equality Act 2010.

D. The actions of the partners amount to direct discrimination under the Equality Act 2010.

E. The actions of the partners amount to positive discrimination under the Equality Act 2010.

Q71 of 90   Flag for review

The claimant is employed at a manufacturing plant as a fitter. The manufacturing plant sub-contracts work to an electrical company. The defendant works for the electrical company. The claimant and defendant have experienced tensions between each other at work and are not on good terms. Last month, both the claimant and the defendant leave work at the same time. On this day, the defendant follows the claimant home and as a practical joke sets off a firework near the claimant as they alight from their car. The firework bounces off the claimant and causes them to fall into the road into the path of an oncoming vehicle, causing them serious personal injury.

Which of the following best describes the liability of the manufacturing plant and/or the electrical company for the claimant's injuries?

A. Neither the manufacturing plant nor the electrical company are vicariously liable for the defendant's dangerous actions as the defendant had deviated from his course of employment.

B. The electrical company is vicariously liable for the defendant's dangerous actions; the manufacturing plant is not vicariously liable as the defendant does not work for the manufacturing plant.

C. The manufacturing plant is vicariously liable for the defendant's dangerous actions as there was sufficient proximity from the defendant leaving work, following the claimant and throwing the firework; the electrical company is not vicariously liable for the defendant's actions as the defendant had deviated from his course of employment.

D. Neither the manufacturing plant nor the electrical company are vicariously liable for the defendant's dangerous actions as the claimant's fall into the road breaks the chain of causation.

E. The manufacturing plant and electrical company are equally vicariously liable for the defendant's dangerous actions.

Flag for review 🏳

A housing association is the owner of a block of flats. The housing association entered into a contract with a company to refurbish the flats. The company sub-contracts the work to a set of builders. Before the work was completed, the company realised that the builders were not going to complete the work on time. To avoid the operation of a penalty clause in their contract with the housing association, the company promised the builders an additional £10,000 if the work was completed on time. The builders completed the work on time. The builders then claimed the additional £10,000 from the company. The company refused to pay the additional amount.

Is the company liable to pay the additional £10,000 to the builders?

A. Yes, as the builders relied on the company's promise of an additional £10,000. This will bind the company to their promise of an additional £10,000.

B. Yes, as the builders completed the work on time, the company avoided the disbenefit of the penalty clause. This will be sufficient consideration to bind the company to their promise of an additional £10,000.

C. No, as the builders were only performing in accordance with their existing contractual duty. This is insufficient consideration to bind the company to their promise of an additional £10,000.

D. Yes, as the builders have exceeded their contractual duty. This is sufficient consideration to bind the company to their promise of an additional £10,000.

E. No, as the builders' consideration is in the past. This is insufficient consideration to bind the company to their promise of an additional £10,000.

Flag for review 🏳

A man is a director and shareholder in a client company. Since its incorporation, the company has operated from a property owned by the man. The company is to buy the property for its market value of £860,000. The company has unamended model articles as its articles of association.

Which of the following statements provides the best description of the process around the successful completion of the transaction?

A. The man will not be permitted to vote at any meeting of the directors or shareholders of the company on any resolution concerning the purchase of the property unless the articles of association are amended.

B. The purchase of the property will need to be approved by an ordinary resolution of the company because the transaction is a substantial property transaction.

C. As the man is a director of the company, if the purchase of the property is not approved by an ordinary resolution of the company before it is entered into, the purchase of the property will be void.

D. Under the Companies Act 2006, the man, as a director of the company, does not need to make a declaration of interest, since exemptions will certainly apply in relation to the proposed purchase of the property.

E. The transaction, whilst of substantial value, will not amount to a substantial property transaction as it does not fall within the definition laid down in the Companies Act 2006.

Q74 of 90   Flag for review 🏳

A solicitor is approached by a client regarding a complex tax issue. The solicitor is unsure of how to handle the case and seeks the assistance of another colleague who is a tax expert. By including the other colleague in the case, the costs for the work done will increase.

Which of the following most accurately describes the obligation on the solicitor?

A. The solicitor is not required to inform the client of any increase in costs.

B. The solicitor must inform the client of any increase in costs.

C. The solicitor is not required to inform the client of any increase in costs as the fees for the other colleague do not amount to costs.

D. The solicitor must inform the client of any substantial increase in costs.

E. The solicitor is not required to inform the client of any increase in costs as the client was provided with information on costs at the time of engagement.

Q75 of 90   Flag for review 🏳

Following the death of a cyclist in a city centre, a large group of cyclists decide to organise a procession in the city centre. Their aim is to attract attention to a campaign which calls for increased road safety measures to be implemented in major city centres to help protect cyclists.

Which of the following statements most accurately describes the notice requirements for such a procession?

A. The notice period is not less than 14 clear days before the date when the procession is intended to be held.

B. The notice period is not less than 24 hours before the date when the procession is intended to be held.

C. The notice period is not less than 21 clear days before the date when the procession is intended to be held.

D. The notice period is not less than six clear days before the date when the procession is intended to be held.

E. The notice period is not less than seven clear days before the date when the procession is intended to be held.

Q76 of 90   Flag for review 🏳

A sole trader has sought advice from a solicitor to assist them in assessing their liability to income tax.

Which of the following can the sole trader exclude from their calculation of their total income for this purpose?

A. Profits from share of partnership business.   ☐

B. Dividends received from a public limited company.   ☐

C. Profit from sale of business premises.   ☐

D. Interest on savings with a building society.   ☐

E. Money received as a result of renting out a property.   ☐

Q77 of 90   Flag for review 🏳

A solicitor is preparing a legal contract for their client who is engaging in the sale of goods with a company. The contract includes a dispute resolution clause that requires any disputes between the client and the company to be resolved through arbitration rather than through court proceedings. The solicitor considers this clause to be disadvantageous to their client's interests.

Which of the following most accurately describes the action that the solicitor should take?

A   The solicitor should amend the dispute resolution clause without informing   ☐
    their client.

B   The solicitor should proceed with the contract without amending the dispute   ☐
    resolution clause or informing their client.

C   The solicitor should inform their client of the potential drawbacks of the dispute ☐
    resolution clause and take instructions on how to proceed.

D   The solicitor should proceed with the contract without amending the dispute   ☐
    resolution clause and inform their client after the fact.

E   The solicitor should amend the dispute resolution clause and inform their client after ☐
    the fact.

Q78 of 90   Flag for review 🏳

A defendant is served with a claim form and particulars of claim. There are some inconsistencies between the nature of the allegations made and facts put forward in the brief details of claim on the claim form and the particulars of claim.

Which of the following best represents how the defendant should proceed?

A. The defendant should deny all allegations in the particulars of claim that they do not admit. The burden of proof is on the claimant to prove the allegations stated. ☐

B. The defendant should deny all allegations in the claim form that they do not admit. The burden of proof is on the claimant to prove the allegations stated. ☐

C. The defendant should ignore any allegations that are inconsistent between the two documents. The burden of proof is on the claimant to prove the allegations stated. ☐

D. The defendant should admit or deny the allegations in the particulars of claim that are within their sphere of knowledge and submit non-admissions against the remainder, dealing with allegations that are inconsistent between the two documents. The defendant should state that the claimant is required to prove the allegations that are the subject of the non-admissions. ☐

E. The defendant should admit or deny the allegations in the claim form that are within their sphere of knowledge and submit non-admissions against the remainder. The defendant should state that the claimant is required to prove the allegations that are the subject of the non-admissions. ☐

Q79 of 90   Flag for review 🏳

A client is a company which is facing increasing pressure from their creditors. The board of directors is concerned about making payments to creditors that an insolvency practitioner would later look to overturn.

Which of the following represents the best advice as to what an insolvency practitioner must look for in assessing whether a payment can be set aside?

A. An insolvency practitioner must look for whether the recipient of the payment is a connected person. ☐

B. An insolvency practitioner must look for whether the payment was made within six months of the date of the insolvency. ☐

C. An insolvency practitioner must look for whether it is possible to establish or presume a desire to prefer the recipient. ☐

D. An insolvency practitioner must look for whether the payment was actuated by proper commercial considerations. ☐

E. An insolvency practitioner must look for whether the recipient is put in a better position as a result of the payment. ☐

Q80 of 90

A married couple formed a partnership with a friend to start a new business. However, soon afterwards, the friend entered into a contract on behalf of the partnership for business equipment that was superfluous to requirements.

Which of the following statements best represents the likely position of the partnership?

A. The partnership cannot be liable for the actions of the friend.

B. The partnership will be liable for the actions of the friend who acted with ostensible authority.

C. The partnership will be liable for the actions of the friend if the friend acted with actual authority.

D. The partnership cannot be liable for the actions of the friend unless all three partners agreed to the contract.

E. The partnership will be liable for the actions of the friend who acted with implied authority.

Q81 of 90

A claimant issues proceedings against a defendant for breach of contract. The losses claimed are £225,000. The defendant files a defence. Shortly after the defence is filed, the claimant discovers from a friend who frequents the defendant's local pub that the defendant is seeking to transfer their house, their only asset, to their son for a fraction of its market value.

Which of the following best represents the steps the claimant should take?

A. The claimant should apply for a freezing injunction with notice. The defendant is entitled to the opportunity to explain their position to the court.

B. The claimant should apply for a freezing injunction with notice. A court hearing will be scheduled quickly, and the defendant will not have sufficient time to dispose of the asset before the hearing.

C. The claimant cannot do anything. The defendant is free to deal with their property howsoever they wish.

D. The claimant should apply for a freezing injunction without notice. The claimant has sufficient evidence to show that there is a real risk of the defendant attempting to dispose of assets in order to avoid payment of any judgment sum.

E. The claimant should apply for a freezing injunction without notice. A with-notice application runs the risk that a court hearing will not be scheduled sufficiently quickly, allowing the defendant to dispose of the asset before the hearing.

The claimant suffers personal injury when a necessary medical procedure is performed negligently. The defendant has conceded liability and admitted negligence. The claimant seeks to claim for loss of earnings, care expenses and DIY costs. Due to the defendant's negligence, the claimant loses the use of their left hand. The claimant was a delivery driver and has been retained by their employer as a customer services operative due to their long-term injuries. The claimant also wants to claim the cost of haircuts (two per year for the next 40 years) due to the accident, as they are now in a customer-facing role and feel their appearance is more important. The client has established hair loss.

Which of the following best describes the court's likely view of the claimant's claim in relation to the haircuts?

A. The court is likely to award an amount but will reduce it by a percentage depending on the claimant's life expectancy.

B. The court will only award damages for future haircutting costs if it is evidenced by a hairdressing specialist.

C. The court will not award any damages for haircutting costs as the claimant would need haircuts in any event and the cost is not as a consequence of the accident.

D. The court will not award any damages for haircutting costs as the claimant did not need to change their job due to the accident.

E. The court is likely to award an amount for haircuts but reduce it by a significant amount due to the claimant's established hair loss.

The Withdrawal Agreement, which removed the UK from the European Union (EU) gives the Trade and Co-Operation Agreement (TCA) legal effect in English law.

In respect of parliamentary sovereignty, which of the following statements most accurately describes the status of the TCA in English law?

A. Parliament has permitted the EU to legislate for the UK for the limited purposes of the TCA. Parliament cannot withdraw this permission under any circumstances.

B. The TCA has legal effect in the UK but gives domestic courts the power to disapply any of its provisions.

C. Parliament has permitted the EU to legislate for the UK for the limited purposes of the TCA. Parliament could withdraw this permission through an Act of Parliament if it chooses to do so.

D. The TCA has legal effect in the UK but is not binding and Parliament can choose to disapply any of its provisions because the UK is no longer a member of the EU.

E. Parliament has permitted the EU to legislate for the UK for the limited purposes of the TCA but it may overrule any aspect of EU law if it chooses to do so.

Flag for review

A large group of animal rights protestors are taking part in a demonstration outside a fashion store that sells real animal furs. The store is located on a very narrow street in a city centre. The demonstration quickly becomes chaotic. The police are concerned that the demonstration may be out of control and may lead to serious disorder. As such, the police wish to instruct the protestors to move their demonstration to a wider nearby street.

Which of the following statements most accurately describes the power of the police?

A   The police may instruct the protestors to move their demonstration where there is a reasonable belief that the demonstration may result in serious disorder.   ☐

B   The police do not have the power to instruct the protestors to move their demonstration unless a public order offence has been committed.   ☐

C   The police may instruct the protestors to move their demonstration where they believe it is reasonable and necessary.   ☐

D   The protestors enjoy an absolute right to freedom of assembly so the police cannot instruct the protestors to move their demonstration.   ☐

E.   The police may only instruct the protestors to move their demonstration where appropriate notice is given to the protestors.   ☐

Flag for review

The claimant is a passenger in the defendant's vehicle. One evening the claimant meets the defendant in a local public house and drinks alcohol with the defendant over a number of hours. Later that evening, the defendant offers to drive the claimant home. The claimant accepts and, during the drive, the defendant loses control of the car, causing a collision. The defendant is killed and the claimant is seriously injured.

Which of the following best describes the legal position?

A.   Any claim for damages will be defeated by the defence of consent due to the fact that the claimant consented to the defendant driving them home when they knew the defendant had been drinking alcohol.   ☐

B.   Damages for personal injury will be awarded to the claimant but there will be a reduction of 20% for contributory negligence due to the fact that the claimant knew the defendant was intoxicated.   ☐

C.   The court will only award damages for personal injury if the court is satisfied that but for the defendant's negligence the claimant would not have been injured.   ☐

D.   The defence of consent cannot be relied upon as any acceptance by a passenger of the risk associated with an intoxicated driver is invalid.   ☐

E.   The claimant is unable to bring a claim for personal injury against the defendant or their estate as the defendant is deceased.   ☐

Q86 of 90   Flag for review 🏳

A claimant commences proceedings against a defendant for breach of contract. The defendant defends the proceedings but fails to deny any of the claim's legal bases or facts advanced in the particulars of claim.

Which of the following best represents how the claimant should proceed?

A. The claimant should file a reply to the defence, indicating to the court that the defendant has failed to deny either the legal basis of the claim or the material facts upon which the claim is based. ☐

B. The claimant should make an application for summary judgment on the basis that the defendant has failed to deny either the legal basis of the claim or the material facts upon which the claim is based and therefore has no real prospect of successfully defending the claim or that there is no compelling reason why the claim should proceed to trial. ☐

C. The claimant should make an application for summary judgment on the basis that the defendant has failed to deny either the legal basis of the claim or the material facts upon which the claim is based and therefore has no real prospect of successfully defending the claim and there is no other compelling reason why the claim should proceed to trial. ☐

D. The claimant should make an application for default judgment on the basis that the defendant has failed to deny either the legal basis of the claim or the material facts upon which the claim is based and therefore has no real prospect of successfully defending the claim or that there is no compelling reason why the claim should proceed to trial. ☐

E. The claimant should make an application for default judgment on the basis that the defendant has failed to deny either the legal basis of the claim or the material facts upon which the claim is based and therefore has no real prospect of successfully defending the claim and there is no other compelling reason why the claim should proceed to trial. ☐

Q87 of 90   Flag for review 🏳

A solicitor is acting on behalf of the executors of an estate. The estate comprises a range of assets which include shares. The executors explain that they need to sell some of the shares so that they are able to make a distribution. The solicitor duly begins to arrange the sale of the shares.

Which of the following best describes the solicitor's position in respect of compliance with financial services legislation?

A. The solicitor may not act in the sale of the shares unless they seek authorisation from the Financial Conduct Authority. ☐

B. The solicitor may act in the sale of the shares because an exclusion would be applicable. ☐

C. The solicitor may act in the sale of the shares providing the firm they work for is regulated by the Financial Conduct Authority. ☐

D. The solicitor may act in the sale of the shares because legal service providers are classified as authorised persons under financial services legislation. ☐

E. The solicitor may not act in the sale of the shares because none of the exclusions would be applicable in these circumstances. ☐

Q88 of 90   Flag for review

A claimant makes an application for summary judgment against the defendant on the basis that the defence has no real prospect of success. At the hearing, the defendant is able to persuade the court that there is an extremely slim possibility that their defence is more than imaginary.

Which of the following best describes the order that the court is most likely to make?

A. The court will likely make a conditional order, requiring the defendant to file a proper defence setting out their legal and factual position within 14 days of the date of the hearing.

B. The court will likely order judgment on the claim on the basis that both grounds have been made out by the claimant and the overriding objective states that cases should be dealt with at proportionate cost.

C. The court will likely order judgment on the claim on the basis that the defendant's prospect of successfully defending the claim is still close to imaginary.

D. The court will likely dismiss the claimant's application as they have failed to prove both of the required grounds under the Civil Procedure Rules 1998.

E. The court will likely make a conditional order, requiring the defendant to file a proper defence setting out their legal and factual position within 28 days of the date of the hearing.

Q89 of 90   Flag for review

A business entered into a contract with a manufacturer. Under the contract, the manufacturer was to supply an electricity generator to the business. The contract stated the delivery date as 1 May.

Due to a shortage of delivery drivers, the generator was delivered ten days late. The late delivery caused the business £10,000 loss of ordinary business profit. The business could have hired a replacement generator in the meantime, which would have reduced its loss by 50%, but the business did not want to spend any further money.

In a claim for breach of contract, which of the following statements best describes the damages the business is likely to recover from the manufacturer?

A. The business could recover the actual loss caused by the breach of contract, as the loss was a natural consequence of the breach.

B. The business could only recover those damages that were in the reasonable contemplation of the defendant at the time the contract was formed.

C. The business could recover the actual loss, subject to an appropriate deduction if the business failed to reasonably mitigate its loss.

D. The business could recover damages representing their loss of expectation.

E. The business could recover damages that were reasonably foreseeable by the manufacturer.

Q90 of 90   Flag for review 🏳

A solicitor is acting for a claimant in a personal injury dispute. At trial, the claimant's medical expert witness gives evidence that exaggerates the extent of the claimant's injuries.

Which of the following best describes the course of conduct that the solicitor should take?

A. The solicitor should take no action; it is not the solicitor's responsibility to control what the witness says.   ☐

B. The solicitor should speak to the medical expert witness after the proceedings and advise them that their evidence was exaggerated.   ☐

C. The solicitor should inform the court of the exaggeration in the medical evidence.   ☐

D. The solicitor should advise the claimant to find a new medical expert witness for future court appearances.   ☐

E. The solicitor should ask the medical expert witness to provide a more accurate assessment of the claimant's injuries.   ☐

■ REFLECTION

CANDIDATE INSTRUCTIONS

Session 1 has now ended. In the real SQE1 assessment, once Session 1 has ended you cannot return to it during the break or during Session 2.

In the SQE1 assessment, you will now be given a break of one hour before Session 2 begins. During this break you may leave the test centre. You are advised to return to the test centre after 50 minutes to ensure that the security checks can be carried out in time for you to commence Session 2 on time.

We advise that you follow the same timings for this simulated SQE-style assessment, and now take a one-hour break.

PAUSE TO REFLECT

You could use the break from your assessment as an opportunity for reflection. Ask yourself the reflective questions in Table 3.

Table 3: Reflecting on FLK1 Session 1 MCQs

How did you find the MCQs in Session 1?	• Did you find them to be easy? • Did you find them to be challenging? Why was this? • Did you flag any for review? If so, what was troubling you about the MCQ?
How confident were you with the MCQs?	• Did you know the answers? • Did you guess any? If so, do you need to revisit your substantive knowledge of the FLK subjects? • Can you identify any particular FLK subjects that you found easier or harder than other subjects?
Did you manage to complete all 90 MCQs in the time permitted?	• Did you manage your time well? • Did you end up with time left over at the end, or did you have to rush? • Did you keep an eye on the clock at regular times during the assessment?
How did you approach the MCQs?	• Did you know some answers straight away? • Did you read the MCQ in full twice before choosing an answer, or did it take you more attempts at reading the MCQ?

In asking yourself these questions, we hope that you will appreciate that there is a skill involved in approaching MCQs as a form of assessment. Refer back to the Introduction to consider whether your approach to MCQs is working for you. Do you need to alter your approach? For example, if you did not manage to complete 90 questions in the allocated time, consider keeping a closer eye on your clock during Session 2.

RETURN FOR SESSION 2

When you return from your scheduled break, remove all distractions and prepare for Session 2.

Once you are ready to commence Session 2 of *Prepare for SQE1: FLK1 Practice Assessment*, set a timer for 2 hours, 33 minutes: click the start button and begin (questions overleaf).

Session 2 questions

A claimant commences proceedings against a defendant for the sum of £21,000, inclusive of £3,500 in interest. In the defendant's defence, they admit to owing the claimant the sum of £8,500 but deny owing the remainder.

Which of the following best represents the position the court will likely adopt when allocating the claim to an appropriate track?

A. The court is likely to allocate the claim to the fast track on the basis that its financial value is below £25,000.

B. The court is likely to allocate the claim to the fast track on the basis of its complexity.

C. The court is likely to allocate the claim to the small claims track on the basis that its financial value is below £10,000.

D. The court is likely to allocate the claim to the small claims track on the basis of its complexity.

E. The court is likely to allocate the claim to the small claims track on the basis that the trial will last less than half a day.

A solicitor is dealing with an estate that includes company shares, gilts and investment property.

Which of the following statements most accurately describes the assets in the estate?

A. The company shares, gilts and investment property are classified as specified investments under financial services legislation.

B. None of the assets listed are classified as specified investments under financial services legislation.

C. Only the company shares and investment property are classified as specified investments under financial services legislation.

D. Only the gilts and investment property are classified as specified investments under financial services legislation.

E. Only the company shares and gilts are classified as specified investments under financial services legislation.

Flag for review 🏳

A shareholder is planning to transfer their shares in a company to a third party. This third party wishes to ensure that the necessary formalities to transfer the legal ownership of the shares are complied with.

Which of the following must occur if the third party is to become the legal owner of the shares?

A. The name of the recipient is entered into the Register of Members.   ☐

B. There is a board resolution to approve the transfer.   ☐

C. The company secretary files a Return on Transfer of Shares at Companies House after the transfer.   ☐

D. The articles of association must be checked for any restrictions on transfer.   ☐

E. The Stock Transfer Form is sent to the Stamp Office.   ☐

Flag for review 🏳

During the negotiations for the purchase of a coffee shop, the seller stated that there were no other coffee shops within a five-mile radius of the business. Shortly after the sale was concluded, the buyer discovered that there were in fact two coffee shops within a five-mile radius. Keen to make a success of the business, the buyer conducted a promotional campaign and lowered the prices of all products sold by the coffee shop.

Six months after the promotional campaign, the coffee shop was still losing money and the buyer brought a claim for misrepresentation against the seller and rescission of the contract.

If successful in the claim for misrepresentation, can the buyer rescind the contract?

A. No, as rescission is only available for a fraudulent misrepresentation, and there is no overt evidence of fraud on the facts.   ☐

B. No, as the statement by the seller did not induce the buyer to purchase the coffee shop.   ☐

C. Yes, as rescission is generally available for all types of misrepresentation.   ☐

D. No, as upon discovering the truth of the misrepresentation, the buyer has affirmed the contract.   ☐

E. Yes, as the seller sought to rescind the contract within a reasonable time.   ☐

Flag for review 🏳

A solicitor is dealing with a case in the Court of Appeal. The Court of Appeal reached its decision by distinguishing it from the Supreme Court.

Which of the following statements most accurately describes the status of the Supreme Court authority?

A. The effect of the Court of Appeal decision is that the Supreme Court authority remains good law and may be followed by inferior courts.   ☐

B. The effect of the Court of Appeal decision is that the Supreme Court authority is now persuasive precedent rather than a binding precedent.   ☐

C. The effect of the Court of Appeal decision is that the Supreme Court authority was overturned and may not be relied on in future cases.   ☐

D. The effect of the Court of Appeal decision is that the Supreme Court authority remains a binding precedent on all inferior courts.   ☐

E. The effect of the Court of Appeal decision is that the Supreme Court authority is no longer good law.   ☐

Flag for review 🏳

A man purchased a second-hand motorcycle from a woman. The woman stated that the motorcycle was a 2015 model. Shortly after the purchase, the man discovered that the motorcycle was a 2005 model, and as such was worth considerably less than he paid. The man brings a claim for misrepresentation against the woman.

What are the key elements of an actionable misrepresentation in the law of contract?

A. A fraudulent statement that results in loss or damage.   ☐

B. A false statement of fact that induces another party to enter into a contract.   ☐

C. A false statement of fact or opinion that induces another party to enter into a contract.   ☐

D. A misleading statement of opinion that was made negligently or recklessly and was reasonably relied upon by the other party.   ☐

E. A false statement, the truth of which could not reasonably have been discovered by the other party.   ☐

Session 2 questions

Flag for review ⚑

A solicitor represents a client in a small claims court. During the trial, the District Judge asks the solicitor a question to which the solicitor does not know the answer. In response, the solicitor provides a lengthy and irrelevant explanation, causing the trial to go on longer than necessary.

What should the solicitor do in this situation?

A. The solicitor should continue to provide a lengthy and irrelevant answer to the District Judge's question unless they think of the correct answer to give. ☐

B. The solicitor should apologise to the District Judge, explain that they do not know the answer to the question, and request a brief adjournment to research the answer. ☐

C. The solicitor should give an answer to the District Judge that they know to be incorrect in order to avoid wasting court time. ☐

D. The solicitor should apologise to the District Judge, explain that they do not know the answer to the question. ☐

E. The solicitor should cease to act for the client. ☐

Flag for review ⚑

An Act of Parliament ('the Act') has recently been enacted, receiving Royal Assent on 21 January 2023.

Following the short title of the Act, the following words are present:

'The Act includes a specific commencement date of 11 March 2023 but the commencement date for section 1 of the Act is yet to be appointed.'

Which of the following statements most accurately describes the day on which the Act comes into force?

A. All sections of the Act came into force on the date it received Royal Assent. ☐

B. Most sections of the Act came into force on the commencement date but section 1 of the Act will only come into effect when it has been enacted by a statutory instrument. ☐

C. All sections of the Act came into force on the enactment date. ☐

D. Most sections of the Act came into force on the commencement date but section 1 of the Act will only come into effect when it has been enacted by the enacting formula. ☐

E. All sections of the Act came into force on the commencement date. ☐

Flag for review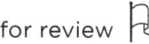

The claimant and defendant are breaking into a bank vault. In order to remove the door of the bank vault to access the gold bullion stored in the bank, the defendant uses dynamite to blow the locks off the door of the vault. The defendant fails to tell the claimant that they intend to use explosives and as a result the claimant is seriously injured in the explosion that ensues.

What is the likely view of the court in respect of the claimant's claim for personal injury against the defendant?

A. The court is unlikely find the defendant at fault as the claimant consented to trying to steal from the bank.

B. The court is likely to find the defendant at fault due to their negligent actions.

C. The court is unlikely to find the defendant at fault as the claimant's injuries are not directly connected to the defendant's actions.

D. The court is likely to find the defendant at fault but reduce the claimant's damages in respect of contributory negligence.

E. The court is unlikely to find the defendant at fault as there is a very close connection between the illegal activity of breaking into the bank and the claimant's injury suffered as a result.

Flag for review

A supplier of food packaging had a contract to supply packaging to a retail business. The retail business was the supplier's most valuable customer, accounting for approximately 80% of the supplier's business.

The supplier entered into a contract with a haulage company. The haulage company agreed to deliver goods from the supplier to the retail business. One day before the delivery was due to take place, the haulage company informed the supplier that they would not make the delivery as the terms of the contract did not provide the haulage company with sufficient profit. The haulage company demanded an additional 40% of the contract price from the supplier. If the supplier did not agree, then the haulage company would not make the delivery as scheduled.

Fearing that late delivery would irrevocably damage the ongoing relationship with the retail business a loss that the supplier could not withstand, and unable to find another company to make the delivery the supplier agreed to pay the additional amount. The haulage company made the delivery as agreed and claimed the additional 40% from the supplier. The supplier refused to pay the additional amount

In a claim by the haulage company against the supplier for the additional amount, which of the following best describes the most likely outcome?

A. The supplier is not bound by their promise of the additional 40% as this was not supported by consideration.

B. The supplier is bound by their promise of the additional 40% as the haulage company, by making the delivery on time, conferred a practical benefit to the supplier.

C. The supplier is bound by their promise of the additional 40% as the supplier avoided the disbenefit of breaching their contract with the retail customer.

D. The supplier is bound by their promise of the additional 40% as damages would provide them with an adequate legal remedy.

E. The supplier is not bound by their promise of the additional 40% as, in the circumstances, the supplier had no realistic alternative but to promise the additional amount.

Flag for review

The claimant works for a cleaning company that contracts their services to different organisations. One of the organisations is a ferry company that owns a number of ferries and vessels. The claimant is instructed by their employers to attend at the local ferry port to clean a ferry for their employer's clients. On arriving at the port, the claimant approaches to embark on the ferry and due to a gap in the gangway, trips and breaks their ankle.

What is the likely outcome of a claim brought against the claimant's employers by the claimant for personal injury?

A. The claim will likely fail on the basis that the employer was not at fault for the gangway leading to the ferry.

B. The claim will likely succeed but the court will reduce the claimant's damages by a percentage to reflect contributory negligence.

C. The claim will likely fail on the basis that the employer could not have foreseen the risk to the claimant as they embarked onto the ferry.

D. The claim will likely succeed on the basis that the claimant's employer owes a duty to the claimant to provide a safe place of work.

E. The claim will likely fail on the basis that the employer has delegated their duties to the ferry company and as a consequence is not liable for the claimant's injuries.

Flag for review

A solicitor is instructed by a client in the sale of their business. During the course of the transaction, the solicitor recommends a financial advisor to the client. The financial advisor agrees to pay the solicitor a referral fee of £1,000 for the introduction. The solicitor has not informed the client of this fact.

What is the solicitor's duty under the SRA Code of Conduct in respect of the referral fee?

A. The solicitor must notify the client of the referral fee and obtain their consent to receive it.

B. The solicitor does not need to disclose the referral fee to the client as it is a separate business arrangement.

C. The solicitor does not need to disclose the referral fee to the client as it is for a small amount of money.

D. The solicitor must notify the client of the referral fee, but may receive it without the client's consent.

E. The solicitor does not need to disclose the referral fee to the client as the fee is not related to the legal services provided by the solicitor.

Q13 of 90   Flag for review 🏴

A large commercial law firm has been approached by a potential client. The client is a man who wishes to instruct the solicitor in respect of a one-off transaction worth £10,000. The firm has no pre-existing business relationship with the client.

Which of the following statements most accurately describes the steps the firm must take to comply with anti-money laundering regulations?

A. The firm must verify the client's identity using their passport.

B. The firm must follow standard customer due diligence requirements because the client is instructing the solicitors in respect of an occasional transaction.

C. The firm must follow enhanced due diligence requirements.

D. The firm does not need to follow customer due diligence requirements because the value of the transaction does not exceed the relevant threshold.

E. The firm must follow standard customer due diligence requirements because a new business relationship is being formed between the firm and the client.

Q14 of 90   Flag for review 🏴

A company wishes to remove one of its directors on the grounds of poor performance of their duties.

Which of the following best describes the procedure for removal of a director?

A. The director was appointed by the board of directors, so they can be removed in the same way. Companies House must be notified and the Register of Directors updated.

B. The director's removal will need any weighted voting clause to be disapplied before the shareholders pass an ordinary resolution to remove them.

C. The director can be removed by the shareholders passing a special resolution on 28 days' notice. Companies House must be notified and the Register of Directors updated.

D. The board must call a shareholders' meeting to pass an ordinary resolution. Companies House must be notified and the Register of Directors updated.

E. The director will automatically be removed as a director when their service contract is terminated by the board of directors. Companies House must be notified and the Register of Directors updated.

Flag for review ⚑

The Secretary of State for Health wishes to implement new regulations to help to combat the spread of a contagious virus. Neither House of Parliament objects to the regulations.

Which of the following statements most accurately describes the Secretary of State's legal position?

A. The Secretary of State may implement such regulations with the consent of the House of Commons and the House of Lords. ☐

B. The Secretary of State may implement such regulations providing they have been given the power to introduce such regulations under an enabling or parent Act. ☐

C. The Secretary of State may implement such regulations if the health and safety of the public is at risk. ☐

D. The Secretary of State does not have the power to implement such regulations. ☐

E. The Secretary of State may implement such regulations with the consent of the Prime Minister. ☐

Flag for review ⚑

The claimant and their family are visiting a stately home on an old country estate. The stately home was built over 200 years ago, and certain areas are undergoing renovation. The claimant wishes to visit the toilets and sees a shortcut down a corridor. There is warning sign hanging from the ceiling in the corridor which reads 'DANGER'. As the claimant is walking along the corridor, a defective floorboard gives way, causing the claimant to be injured. In their defence, the stately home plead that the 'DANGER' sign referred to the inadequate flooring in the corridor.

Which of the following best describes the court's likely view as to the stately home's defence?

A. The defence will likely fail on the basis that the warning is not specific enough, nor does it refer to the floorboards which would alert visitors to the issue with the uneven floor. ☐

B. The defence will likely succeed on the basis that the stately home gave a warning to visitors. ☐

C. The defence will likely fail on the basis that the claimant was a trespasser as they were using a shortcut which was not accessible due to the dangerous state of the corridor. ☐

D. The defence will likely succeed if the court finds that there was a significant risk incidental to the claimant using the shortcut to the toilet. ☐

E. The defence will likely fail but the claimant will be found contributorily negligent on the basis they failed to heed the warning sign. ☐

Q17 of 90   Flag for review

A man died leaving a valid will in which he stated that his wife can live in the matrimonial home for the rest of her life. The executors of the will formed an agreement with the wife under which she could live in the property for the rest of her life, providing that she paid £1 per year rent. Several months later, the other members of the man's family challenged this agreement on the basis that £1 per year was not a sufficient market rate to allow her to live in the property.

Can the woman enforce the agreement with the executors?

A. Yes, as the woman has relied upon the promise of the executors.

B. No, as payment of £1 per year is not adequate as consideration.

C. Yes, as payment of £1 per year is sufficient consideration.

D. No, as payment of £1 per year has minimal economic value.

E. No, as the woman's consideration was in the past.

Q18 of 90   Flag for review

Two brothers own a business in partnership. They have just sold their premises which has doubled in value. The two brothers are looking to buy an industrial unit so that they can expand their business.

Which of the following provides the best advice in relation to the brothers' Capital Gains Tax (CGT) position?

A. The two brothers will be liable to pay CGT on the disposal of the shop premises.

B. The two brothers' liability to pay CGT will be postponed by electing to roll over their gain into new premises using Business Asset Rollover Relief.

C. The two brothers' CGT bills will each be reduced by their £12,000 Annual Exempt Amount.

D. The two brothers' liability to pay CGT will be postponed by electing to hold over their gain using Holdover Relief.

E. The two brothers' liability to pay CGT will be extinguished by electing to roll over their gain into new premises using Business Asset Rollover Relief.

Flag for review 🏳

The Supreme Court hears an appeal concerning a clinical negligence claim. At first instance, the High Court found in favour of the defendant. The Court of Appeal (Civil Division) also found in favour of the defendant. The Supreme Court determines that the High Court and Court of Appeal (Civil Division) have misapplied the relevant legal principle and rules in favour of the claimant.

Which of the following statements most accurately describes the effect of the decision of the Court of Appeal (Civil Division)?

A. The Court of Appeal (Civil Division) decision would still be binding on all inferior courts because the Court of Appeal is above inferior courts in the court hierarchy. ☐

B. The Court of Appeal (Civil Division) decision has been overturned by the Supreme Court and is no longer binding on inferior courts. ☐

C. The Court of Appeal (Civil Division) decision has been distinguished by the Supreme Court; both decisions are legally binding on inferior courts. ☐

D. The Court of Appeal (Civil Division) decision has been overruled by the Supreme Court and is no longer binding on inferior courts. ☐

E. The Court of Appeal (Civil Division) decision has been reversed by the Supreme Court and is no longer binding on inferior courts. ☐

Flag for review 🏳

The claimant is a business owner attending a conference organised by his employer. The conference is taking place in a large hotel. One morning the claimant uses the lift in the hotel to attend the 9:00am presentation on day two of the conference. Due to a technical fault in the lift mechanism, the lift doors close on the claimant's outstretched arm, breaking his elbow. There is a sign at reception in the hotel that reads: 'The hotel accepts no responsibility for personal injury or death.'

What is the likely outcome of a claim brought against the hotel for the claimant's personal injuries?

A. The claim will likely fail on the basis that the hotel displayed a sign excluding liability for personal injury. ☐

B. The claim will likely succeed on the basis that the hotel is unable to exclude liability for personal injury and the accident has been caused by the state of the premises. ☐

C. The claim will likely fail on the basis that the accident is an unforeseen consequence of the claimant using the lift. ☐

D. The claim will likely succeed on the basis that the claimant was a non-consumer and the hotel owed them a duty of care. ☐

E. The claim will likely fail on the basis that the claimant is a visitor to the premises and their injury has not been caused by the state of the premises, only the premature closing of the lift doors. ☐

Flag for review 🏳

A man sells his only property to a woman for £100,000. The market value of the property is £500,000. The woman is a physician, and the man is one of her patients. The man's family members were concerned when they heard about the sale and encouraged the man to seek legal advice. A solicitor advised the man that the sale should be set aside as a result of undue influence.

Which of the following statements best explains the legal position?

A. The sale, whilst under market value, is legally binding as the woman's payment of £100,000 constitutes valuable consideration. ☐

B. The sale may be set aside because of actual undue influence exerted by the woman over the man. ☐

C. The sale may be set aside but only if the man can produce sufficient evidence that the sale was a result of undue influence applied by the woman. ☐

D. The sale may be set aside as the relationship between the man and the woman is one of trust and confidence. ☐

E. The sale of the house is a transaction that calls for explanation and the relationship creates a rebuttable presumption of influence. The woman will need to rebut the presumption to avoid a finding of undue influence and the contract being set aside. ☐

Flag for review 🏳

Two companies are involved in a dispute over the quality of materials used in a marketing campaign. The value of the claim is £750. The claimant indicates to their solicitor that they would like to rely on two expert reports at a cost of £800 each as well as disclosing copies of over 1,000 emails exchanged between the parties.

Which of the following best represents the advice the solicitor should give to the claimant in light of the Civil Procedure Rules (CPR) 1998?

A. The claimant should be able to rely on the two expert reports and disclose all of the evidence as the overriding objective of the CPR 1998 states that cases must be dealt with justly and fairly. ☐

B. The claimant should be able to rely on the two expert reports and disclose all of the evidence as the overriding objective of the CPR 1998 states that courts should ensure that parties are placed on an even footing. ☐

C. The overriding objective of the CPR 1998 states that cases should be dealt with in ways that are proportionate to the amount of money involved, so it is unlikely the courts will allow the claimant to rely on the two expert reports and disclose all of the evidence. ☐

D. The overriding objective of the CPR 1998 states that cases should be dealt with in ways that are proportionate to the available court resources, so it is unlikely the courts will allow the claimant to rely on the two expert reports and disclose all of the evidence. ☐

E. The overriding objective of the CPR 1998 states that cases should be dealt with in ways that are proportionate to the complexity of the issues, so it is unlikely the courts will allow the claimant to rely on the two expert reports and disclose all of the evidence. ☐

Q23 of 90   Flag for review 🏳

The European Union (EU) has recently passed a new law concerning healthcare rights. The law was passed in February 2022. The UK exited from the EU on 31 January 2020.

Which of the following statements most accurately describes the status of the EU law in the UK?

A. The EU law concerning healthcare rights has no effect in the UK.   ☐

B. The EU law concerning healthcare rights has vertical effect in the UK.   ☐

C. The EU law concerning healthcare rights has direct effect in the UK.   ☐

D. The EU law concerning healthcare rights has both vertical and direct effect in the UK. ☐

E. The EU law concerning healthcare rights is classified as retained EU law and has effect ☐
    in the UK.

Q24 of 90   Flag for review 🏳

A well-respected children's rights organisation ('the organisation') wishes to make an application for judicial review of a local education authority's decision to change the school uniform policy for schools within its remit.

Which of the following most accurately describes the procedure that the organisation must follow?

A. The organisation must apply to the Administrative Court. It must file the application   ☐
    no later than three months after the grounds to make the claim arose, and must
    be granted leave by demonstrating that the claim is arguable and has a reasonable
    prospect of success.

B. The organisation must apply to the Court of Appeal. It must file the application no later ☐
    than three months after the grounds to make the claim arose, and must be granted
    leave by demonstrating that the claim is arguable and has a reasonable prospect of
    success.

C. The organisation must apply to the Administrative Court. It must file the application no   ☐
    later than six weeks after the grounds to make the claim arose, and must demonstrate
    that the claim is arguable and has a reasonable prospect of success.

D. The organisation must apply to the Court of Appeal. It must file the application no   ☐
    later than three months after the grounds to make the claim arose, and must be
    granted leave by demonstrating that the claim is arguable and has a good prospect
    of success.

E   The organisation must apply to the Administrative Court. It must file the application   ☐
    no later than three months after the grounds to make the claim arose, and must be
    granted leave by demonstrating that the claim is arguable and has a good prospect of
    success.

Q25 of 90   Flag for review

A man is employed as a travelling salesperson. His employer is a specialist supplier of machinery to the agriculture industry. The man's contract with his employer contains a term that upon termination of his contract of employment, the man cannot act as a travelling salesperson in relation to any industry for a period of ten years.

Which of the following statements best explains whether the man is bound by the term of the contract?

A. The man is bound by the term as the clause is reasonably necessary to protect a legitimate interest of the employer.

B. The man is not bound by the term as it is an unreasonable restriction on the livelihood of the man, amounting to a restraint of trade.

C. The man is bound by the term as the term has been freely agreed by both parties.

D. The man is not bound by the term due to illegality. A clause restraining trade is unenforceable.

E. The man is bound by the term in order to protect the trade secrets of the employer.

Q26 of 90   Flag for review

A newly qualified solicitor has been assigned to a new client for the first time. The solicitor has arranged a meeting with the client. A partner in the firm tells the newly qualified solicitor that they know the client well and should not be concerned about performing due diligence checks.

Which of the following accurately describes the duty of the newly qualified solicitor when meeting with the new client?

A. The newly qualified solicitor should accept the oral representations from the client as to their identity and finances.

B. The newly qualified solicitor should ask for the client's identification and verify their information before proceeding.

C. The newly qualified solicitor should proceed with the matter without verifying the client's identification as this is only the first meeting.

D. The newly qualified solicitor should rely on the information provided by the partner of the firm.

E. The newly qualified solicitor should ask the partner to verify the client's identity since the partner knows the client well.

Flag for review 🏳

A client owns 4% of the shares in a private limited company. The company has unamended model articles as its articles of association. On checking the recent accounts of the company, the client is concerned that the directors are effectively paying out all the profits of the company to themselves as directors. The client is not happy about this and seeks advice as to what can be done.

Which of the following is unlikely to be an available option for the client?

A. Request that the directors call an extraordinary general meeting so that the matter can be discussed by all the shareholders in attendance at the meeting.

B. Instigate a derivative action on the basis that the directors' actions amount to a breach of their duties as directors.

C. Seek support from other shareholders owning at least 71% of the shares to pass a special resolution to prevent the directors from paying similar amounts to themselves in the future.

D. Seek support from other shareholders owning more than 46% of the shares to pass an ordinary resolution to remove the directors from office.

E. Apply to the court to require the directors to call an extraordinary general meeting so that the matter can be discussed by all the shareholders in attendance at the meeting.

Flag for review 🏳

A solicitor is acting for a client in a claim. As part of the directions, the court has ordered that witness statements need to be exchanged no later than 4pm on 1 November. The solicitor drafts all of the witness statements, but is called away to court on 1 November and fails to deliver the copies by the deadline. The defendant's witness statements are delivered by hand to the solicitor's reception at 3.58pm on 1 November, and the receptionist informs the solicitor at 4.05pm. In response, the solicitor hand delivers the claimant's witness statement to the defendant at 4.45pm. The solicitor immediately telephones the defendant's representative to propose an extension to the deadline, but this is rejected. The claimant's solicitor therefore issues an application to the court for relief from sanctions on 3 November.

Which of the following statements best represents the position of the court in response to the application for relief from sanctions?

A. The court is likely to reject the claimant's application and refuse relief. The court's role is to enforce compliance with procedural rules and directions.

B. The court is likely to grant the claimant's application for relief from sanctions on the basis that the failure to comply with the directions is neither serious nor significant, but will order the claimant to pay both parties' costs.

C. The court is likely to grant the claimant's application for relief from sanctions on the basis that the failure to comply with the directions is neither serious nor significant, but will make a wasted costs order against the claimant's solicitor for failure to comply with the court ordered direction.

D. The court is likely to grant the claimant's application for relief from sanctions on the basis that there was good reason for the failure to comply with the directions and penalise the defendant's solicitor for unreasonably refusing to agree an extension of time.

E. The court is likely to grant the claimant's application for relief from sanctions on the basis that there was good reason for the failure to comply with the directions, but will insist that both parties pay their own costs in relation to the application.

Q29 of 90   Flag for review 🏳

A solicitor is approached by a colleague in the law firm where they work. The colleague explains that they have witnessed sexual harassment on behalf of the senior partner to a paralegal. They have asked the solicitor for their advice in light of the Solicitors Regulation Authority (SRA) Code of Conduct.

What should the solicitor advise the colleague?

A. The solicitor should advise the colleague not to make any report to the SRA as it may lead to the colleague or the paralegal being subject to detrimental treatment. ☐

B. The solicitor should advise the colleague to speak directly to the senior partner concerned about the alleged sexual harassment. ☐

C. The solicitor should advise the colleague that they will speak directly to the senior partner concerned about the alleged sexual harassment. ☐

D. The solicitor should advise the colleague that the paralegal should speak to the senior partner concerned about the alleged sexual harassment. ☐

E. The solicitor should advise the colleague to make a report to the SRA. ☐

Q30 of 90   Flag for review 🏳

A solicitor recently acted on behalf of a client in respect of a high-value civil claim. The client's claim was successful, and the client was awarded substantial damages. The client has now approached the solicitor seeking investment advice. The solicitor advises the client to 'invest in land for property development purposes'.

Which of the following statements most accurately describes the solicitor's position in respect of financial services legislation?

A. The solicitor is unlikely to have breached financial services regulations because the advice they have provided is generic. ☐

B. The solicitor is likely to have breached financial services regulations because they have advised the client in respect of a specified investment. ☐

C. The solicitor is unlikely to have breached financial services regulations because the advice they have provided was given in the course of wider legal services. ☐

D. The solicitor is likely to have breached financial services regulations because they have provided specific investment advice. ☐

E. The solicitor is unlikely to have breached financial services regulations because the advice they have provided is generic and does not relate to a specified investment. ☐

A firm enters into a Damages Based Agreement (DBA) with a client. The DBA is set at 10%. The client wins the case and is awarded £55,000 in damages, a sum that is significantly lower than anticipated. The other party is ordered to pay £1,000 towards the client's costs.

What is the client's liability in respect of their legal fees?

A.   The client is liable to pay £5,500 from the damages they received.   ☐

B.   Under the terms of the DBA the client is not liable to pay any of the solicitor's costs.   ☐

C.   The client is liable to pay £4,500 from the damages they received.   ☐

D.   The client is not liable to pay the solicitor's fee because the damages awarded were less than anticipated.   ☐

E   The client is liable to pay £1,000 towards the solicitor's costs.   ☐

A solicitor issues proceedings on behalf of their client against a company for breach of contract. The solicitor drafts the client's witness statement and writes to him enclosing it. The client asks for information about the process, specifically what formalities are required and what may be included in the content.

Which of the following should be omitted from the letter of advice to the client?

A.   The witness statement must comply with the formalities required by the Civil Procedure Rules 1998 and should include a statement of truth.   ☐

B.   The statement should, so far as is possible, be expressed in the client's own words.   ☐

C.   The client can only include evidence that they would be allowed to give orally; irrelevant and inadmissible evidence must be excluded.   ☐

D.   The client may use their witness statement to argue the r case and to make observations about the evidence of other witnesses.   ☐

E   The client must indicate which statements are made from their own knowledge and provide the source of any information that is not.   ☐

Q33 of 90   Flag for review 🏳

The Court of Appeal is considering a civil appeal. The appellant's submissions rely on a previous decision of the Court of Appeal (Civil Division). The respondent's submissions rely on a previous decision of the House of Lords. The Court of Appeal decision is more recent than the House of Lords decision.

Which of the following statements most accurately describes how the doctrine of precedent would apply in these circumstances?

A. The Court of Appeal is bound to follow its previous decision because none of the reasons to depart from a previous decision applies.

B. The Court of Appeal is bound to follow the decision of the House of Lords because it is a senior court in the court hierarchy.

C. The Court of Appeal may follow its previous decision because it is more recent than the House of Lords decision.

D. The Court of Appeal may choose which of the decisions to follow because it is no longer bound by House of Lords decisions since the creation of the Supreme Court.

E. The Court of Appeal may choose which of the decisions to follow because one of the reasons to depart from a previous decision applies.

Q34 of 90   Flag for review 🏳

The owners of a ship charted the vessel to a shipping company. The period of the charter was three years and a term of the contract required that the owners provided a vessel that was 'in every way fit for ordinary cargo service'. Shortly after taking delivery, the shipping company had the vessel inspected by their insurance company. The insurance company refused to issue a certificate of insurance as the inadequate safety equipment provided by the owners of the vessel did not meet the minimal legal standards to sail. As a result, the vessel could not be used for cargo service for a period of three months until replacement equipment was eventually provided by the owners of the vessel.

The owners receive communication from the solicitors of the shipping company. The shipping company is seeking to repudiate the agreement and is seeking damages for the loss incurred during the three months the vessel was uninsured and unable to sail.

Which of the following statements best describes the legal position?

A. The breach is likely to be held as a breach of warranty, allowing the shipping company to recover damages, but the agreement is not repudiated.

B. The breach is likely to be held as a breach of condition, allowing the shipping company to repudiate the agreement, and claim damages.

C. The shipping company has the choice to repudiate the agreement, but only if it has taken steps to mitigate its loss.

D. The owners of the vessel are not liable for the breach, as the breach was not within their reasonable control.

E. The contract is frustrated, discharging the parties of future obligations under the contract.

Flag for review 🏳

The claimant is injured when they switch a light on in the changing room of a retail outlet that they are visiting. The owners of the retail outlet have employed a reputable firm of electricians to rewire the retail outlet and it has recently reopened to the public. The claimant suffers a burn injury and pursues a claim against the retail outlet for their injuries.

What is the likely outcome of the claimant's claim for personal injuries brought against the retail outlet?

A. The claim will likely fail on the basis that the claimant consented to the risk of injury when they switched the light on in the changing room.   ☐

B. The claim will likely succeed on the basis that the owners of the retail outlet are unable to delegate their duty to ensure visitors to their premises are safe.   ☐

C. The claim will likely fail on the basis that the owners of the retail outlet instructed competent contractors to rewire the outlet.   ☐

D. The claim will likely succeed on the basis that by inviting the claimant to the premises it was foreseeable that an injury would occur from the faulty wiring.   ☐

E. The claim will likely fail on the basis that burn injuries were not a foreseeable risk to the claimant in using the changing rooms at the retail outlet.   ☐

Flag for review 🏳

The claimant is driving two of his colleagues to work in his new motor car. Unbeknown to the claimant, the car has been manufactured with a fault that causes the engine to cut out when the car reaches a certain speed. As the claimant drives along a dual carriageway, the engine cuts out, causing the car to come to an abrupt standstill. The vehicle behind the car attempts to perform an emergency stop to prevent a collision but collides with the rear of the claimant's motor car. A lorry in the queue of traffic behind the car overturns and leaves the carriageway, colliding into a house at the edge of the road.

Who can bring a claim for personal injury against the manufacturer of the car?

A. The claimant and their passengers.   ☐

B. Only the passengers in the claimant's vehicle.   ☐

C. The claimant, their passengers and the lorry driver.   ☐

D. The claimant, their passengers, the lorry driver and any occupants of the house.   ☐

E. The claimant, their passengers, the occupants of the car directly behind the claimant's car, the lorry driver and any occupants of the house.   ☐

Q37 of 90   Flag for review ⚑

A client wishes to bring a claim against a company for breach of contract. The solicitor advises the client that the case is relatively straightforward and has good prospects of success. The solicitor estimates that the client may be able to recover damages of approximately £52,000.

Which of the following statements most accurately describes the appropriate court to consider the client's case?

A. The case should be commenced in the High Court because the estimated value of the claim is less than £100,000. ☐

B. The case should be commenced in the County Court because the estimated value of the claim is less than £100,000. ☐

C. The client may choose to commence proceedings in the County Court or the High Court, regardless of the value of the claim. ☐

D. The case should be commenced in the High Court because the estimated value of the claim is more than £50,000. ☐

E. The case should be commenced in the County Court because the estimated value of the claim is more than £50,000. ☐

Q38 of 90   Flag for review ⚑

The claimant is a lawyer and works from home, only occasionally going to the office to attend meetings. In the claimant's home office, they have their work laptop, work smartphone, personal computer and personal smartphone. Due to a defective charger purchased by the claimant from a well-known IT retailer, a small fire breaks out, which causes damage to both computers and both phones, and burns the claimant's hand when they attempt to put the fire out.

What is the likely outcome of a claim brought under the Consumer Protection Act 1987 for personal injury and property damage against the IT retailer by the claimant?

A. The claimant will likely be able to claim for personal injury and damage to all property. ☐

B. The claimant will likely be able to claim for personal injury but not damage to property. ☐

C. The claimant will likely be able to claim for personal injury and damage to their personal smartphone and personal computer as long as it exceeds £275. ☐

D. The claimant will likely be able to claim only for the work laptop and work smartphone as long as the value is no more than £275 and personal injury. ☐

E. The claimant will likely be able to claim for the faulty chargers, personal injury and all damage to property irrespective of its value. ☐

Flag for review

A client is a private company limited by shares with unamended model articles of association and has the following shareholders:
- Shareholder A – owns 50% of the ordinary share capital
- Shareholder B – owns 25% of the ordinary share capital
- Shareholder C – owns 20% of the ordinary share capital
- Shareholder D – owns 5% of the ordinary share capital.

In relation to shareholder rights and powers, which of the following statements represents an accurate summary of the law?

A. Shareholder A is a person of significant control, and can pass and block an ordinary resolution.

B. Shareholder A is a person of significant control and can block an ordinary resolution.

C. Shareholder B is a person of significant control and can block a special resolution.

D. Shareholder B is not a person of significant control but can block a special resolution.

E. Shareholder C is a person of significant control but is unable to block a special resolution.

Flag for review

A defendant has a contract with a hotel to landscape the hotel's gardens ready for the official opening on 14 May. The defendant orders 2,000 plants and shrubs to complete the landscaping for the hotel from a third-party supplier, the claimant, for £18,500 to be delivered by 7 May. However, the goods do not arrive until 20 May. The defendant refuses to pay the invoice to the claimant. The claimant issues proceedings in the County Court for the monies due and the defendant responds with a defence stating: 'We dispute the payment. The goods arrived too late so we could not fulfil our contract with the hotel. The terms of the contract were agreed orally at a meeting where our sales director made it clear to the claimant's facilities manager that the plants and shrubs had to be delivered by 7 May to allow time for planting and that time was of the essence.' The claimant applies to the court for an order for summary judgment.

Which of the following answers best describes the likely outcome of the claimant's application for summary judgment?

A. The claimant is likely to succeed in its application because the defendant's defence does not provide sufficient detail for the court to determine the matter.

B. The claimant is likely to fail in their application because the court needs to hear oral evidence from witnesses at trial to determine whether time was of the essence. This is necessary to establish whether there is a compelling reason as to why the matter should proceed to trial.

C. The claimant is likely to fail in their application but only because the information provided in the defence is sufficient to demonstrate that the defendant has a real prospect of successfully defending the claim.

D. The claimant is likely to fail in their application because the matter is too complex and technical to be dealt with at a summary judgment hearing, and this is a compelling reason why the matter should proceed to trial.

E. The court is likely to make a conditional order as it is possible but not probable that the defence will succeed.

Q41 of 90   Flag for review 🏳

A claimant is successful in a breach of contract multi-track claim valued at £475,000 against a defendant. The parties both filed their costs budgets on time before the directions hearing, and the court approved those costs budgets. The claimant's costs budget totalled £150,000. At trial, the court makes a costs order in the claimant's favour with such costs to be assessed on the standard basis. The claimant submits a costs claim in the sum of £345,000, arguing that the litigation has proved more costly than predicted.

Which of the following best represents the position on whether the claimant is likely to recover the full value of their costs?

A.   The claimant will be able to recover the full value of their costs as the overall amount claimed is proportionate to the judgment amount.

B.   The claimant will be able to recover the full value of the costs approved in the costs budget as the amount submitted as part of the costs budget was regarded as being proportionate to the value of the dispute.

C.   The claimant will be able to recover the full value of their costs as the court does not need to take proportionality into consideration when assessing costs in multi-track trials.

D.   The claimant will be able to recover the full value of the costs approved in the costs budget and make an application to be awarded the additional costs as the court does not need to take proportionality into consideration when assessing costs in multi-track trials.

E.   The claimant will be able to recover the full value of the costs approved in the costs budget and make an application to be awarded the additional costs as the court does not need to take proportionality into consideration when assessing costs if a party has been successful in the action overall.

Q42 of 90   Flag for review 🏳

A client seeks advice on a particular business type. The client describes the business as one where the owners of the business are often called members and can be individuals or corporations. Liability is limited to the extent that a member has already contributed to the assets of the business. Important details are notified to Companies House. This type of business medium is a legal entity in its own right. A formal agreement governs the relations between members. Members can be removed by a majority of other members following an agreement between the members that this power exists.

Which of the following is the most accurate statement of the type of business being described by the client?

A.   A traditional partnership.

B.   A public limited company.

C.   A private company limited by shares.

D.   A limited liability partnership.

E.   A private company limited by guarantee.

Flag for review 🏳

A man wishes to make a claim for judicial review of a decision by his local authority. The man owns and runs a taxi company, and is concerned by the fact that the local authority has taken the decision to substantially change the requirements to be granted a taxi driving licence. The man claims that the changes would adversely impact his business and other taxi businesses in the area.

Which of the following statements most accurately describes the likelihood of the man being able to bring a claim for judicial review?

A. The man is unlikely to be regarded as having sufficient interest in the claim because he would not be able to demonstrate that the local authority's decision has impacted a significant proportion of the public.

B. The man is likely to be regarded as having sufficient interest in the claim because the decision impacts his business directly. The local authority would be classified as a public body exercising a public function.

C. The man is unlikely to be regarded as having sufficient interest in the claim because he would not be able to demonstrate that the local authority was exercising a public function.

D. The man is likely to be regarded as having sufficient interest in the claim because his rights have been directly impacted by the local authority's decision. The local authority would be classified as a public body exercising a public function.

E. The man is unlikely to be regarded as having sufficient interest in the claim because he would not be able to demonstrate that the local authority's decision has impacted a right protected by the Human Rights Act 1998.

Flag for review 🏳

The court is being asked to consider whether to award the remedy of specific performance or to grant an injunction.

Which of the following statements is relevant to whether the court will exercise its discretion to make such awards?

A. Specific performance will only be awarded when it is reasonable to do so.

B. An injunction will only be awarded when it would be inequitable not to do so.

C. The court is unlikely to grant either specific performance or an injunction when damages would provide an adequate remedy.

D. The court can only grant an injunction or order specific performance in relation to contracts for the sale of land.

E. The court is likely to grant either specific performance or an injunction in relation to a contract of employment.

Q45 of 90   Flag for review 🏳

A claimant makes a Part 36 offer of £40,000 on 1 March to the defendant to settle their dispute. The offer expires on 22 March. The defendant rejects the offer and the matter proceeds to trial. After considering the evidence, the judge finds in the claimant's favour and damages are awarded against the defendant in the sum of £45,000.

Which of the following best represents the likely order the court will make concerning costs?

A. Unless it is unjust to do so, interest will be payable on the claimant's costs from 23 March onwards at a rate of 1% above base rate. ☐

B. Unless it is unjust to do so, interest will be payable by the defendant on the damages awarded at a rate of up to 10% above base rate from the date of cause of action. ☐

C. Unless it is unjust to do so, a split costs order will be made so the defendant is ordered to pay the costs up to 22 March, and the claimant pays the costs from 23 March up to and including the trial. ☐

D. Unless it is unjust to do so, the defendant will pay the claimant's costs on the standard basis up to 22 March and thereafter, from 23 March, on the indemnity basis. ☐

E. Unless it is unjust to do so, the defendant will pay the claimant's costs on the indemnity basis up to 22 March and thereafter, from 23 March, on the standard basis. ☐

Q46 of 90   Flag for review 🏳

A liquidator of a company is appointed. The company has total assets amounting to £420,850,000 once the liquidator has collected in all available assets. The liquidator has been notified of debts as follows:

• a secured loan of £250,000,000 which is secured by a fixed charge
• preferential debts owed to employees of £3,160,000
• a secured loan which, after ring fencing, secures £130,000,000 by way of a floating charge
• an outstanding corporation tax bill of £23,690,000 owed to HMRC
• rent arrears of £37,000,000
• a loan granted to the company by the wife of one of the directors in the amount of £5,000,000
• trade creditors and other sums owed to ordinary creditors of £10,750,000.

There are no winding-up expenses.

Which of the following percentages best represents the amount in each £1 owed that will be paid to the company's ordinary unsecured creditors?

A. 57.6%. ☐

B. 55.3%. ☐

C. 45.8%. ☐

D. 66.6%. ☐

E. 52.8%. ☐

Flag for review

A claimant is successful in their application for judicial review of their local planning authority's decision to refuse to consider a planning application. The court found that the authority had failed to comply with its statutory duty to consult interested parties.

Which of the following remedies is likely to be the most appropriate in this case?

A.   A quashing order.

B.   An injunction.

C.   A prohibiting order.

D.   Damages.

E.   A mandatory order.

Flag for review

The claimant has lived in their rural property for one year. The claimant is woken nightly by lorries delivering goods to a large warehouse on the outskirts of the claimant's village. The warehouse operator has recently expanded their business interests to include exports, as well as imports.

Which of the following best describes whether the claimant has a claim against the warehouse operator?

A.   A claim in private nuisance would likely fail on the basis that the claimant has lived in the area for only a short period of time.

B.   A claim in public nuisance would likely succeed on the basis that the warehouse operator has increased their trade and the frequency of the lorries is interfering with the public's enjoyment.

C.   A claim under the rule in *Rylands v Fletcher* would likely succeed on the basis that the warehouse operator's use of the land and roads are non-natural.

D.   A claim in private nuisance would likely succeed as the frequency and noise of the lorries at night represent an unreasonable interference with the claimant's reasonable enjoyment of their property.

E.   A claim in private nuisance would likely fail on the basis that the claimant has come to the nuisance.

A judge is considering a criminal law case concerning possession of a weapon in a public place. The legislation prescribing the offence provides that 'It is an offence to possess a firearm in a public place without lawful authority to do so'. The legislation also states that 'The term firearm refers to a rifle, pistol, pellet gun, stun gun, handgun, shotgun, or other similar weapons'. The defendant is charged with possession of an air rifle in a public place.

Which of the following statements most accurately identifies how the rules of language are likely to apply in this case?

A. The *ejusdem generis* rule would apply. The air rifle is likely to be deemed to be a weapon under the Act because it is similar to the other weapons listed in the section.

B. The *expressio unius est exclusio alterius* rule would apply. The air rifle is unlikely to be deemed to be a weapon under the Act because it is not expressly listed as a weapon in the section.

C. None of the rules of language are likely to apply in this case.

D. The *ejusdem generis* rule would apply. The air rifle is unlikely be deemed to be a weapon under the Act because it is not sufficiently similar to the other weapons listed in the provision.

E. The *noscitur a sociis* rule would apply. The air rifle is likely to be deemed to be a weapon under the Act because it is clear from the wording of the section that an air rifle is a weapon within the meaning of the Act.

The claimant's business property is destroyed when a neighbouring building explodes. The neighbouring building was used to store gas canisters. The owner of the building had failed to appreciate that the canisters needed to be used within a limited period of time. Storing the canisters beyond their expiry date has caused them to react with the air and explode.

Which of the following best describes the legal position?

A. The claimant is likely to be able to bring a claim pursuant to *Rylands v Fletcher* as their neighbour has brought something onto the land that escaped and was foreseeable to cause harm in doing so.

B. The claimant is unlikely to be able to bring a claim pursuant to *Rylands v Fletcher* as the explosion is an inevitable accident and not foreseeable.

C. The claimant is likely to be able to bring a claim in private nuisance as the explosion is an unreasonable interference with the claimant's enjoyment of their property.

D. The claimant is unlikely to be able to bring a claim pursuant to *Rylands v Fletcher* as the explosion is an isolated incident.

E. The claimant is likely to be able to bring a claim in public nuisance as the storing of expired canisters has caused unreasonable interference with a class of people, namely the claimant's neighbours.

Flag for review 🏳

A solicitor is acting on behalf of a client who believes that the law governing the pension rights afforded to cohabitees violates their human rights. The client wants the offending statutory provision to be declared void.

Which of the following statements best describes the court's power to make such a ruling?

A. The Supreme Court can make a ruling that declares a statutory provision to be void because it breaches human rights legislation. ☐

B. The High Court, Court of Appeal and Supreme Court may make a declaration that a statutory provision is incompatible with human rights legislation, but they do not have the power to declare that a statutory provision is void. ☐

C. The High Court, Court of Appeal and Supreme Court may make a declaration that a statutory provision is void because it breaches human rights legislation. ☐

D. Only the European Court of Human Rights has the power to declare that specific provisions of domestic legislation are void if they breach human rights legislation. ☐

E. The Court of Appeal and Supreme Court may make a declaration that a statutory provision is void because it breaches human rights legislation. ☐

Flag for review 🏳

A man entered into a 12-month lease of a property. The terms of the lease required the man to provide a guarantor in the event that the man failed to pay the rent.

Eight months into the lease, the landlord is now bringing a claim against the guarantor as the man has failed to pay the rent for the last six months.

Which of the following statements best explains the legal position and whether the landlord can claim the arrears from the guarantor?

A. The guarantor is under a primary obligation to pay the arrears. The landlord can choose whether to enforce the claim against the man or the guarantor. ☐

B. The guarantor is under secondary obligation to pay the arrears. To enforce the guarantee, the landlord must have first claimed and failed to recover the arrears from the man. ☐

C. The guarantor is only liable for the arrears if the terms of the original agreement are unenforceable. ☐

D. The guarantor is only liable for the arrears once the 12 months of the lease have expired. ☐

E. The guarantor is only liable for the rent due in the four months remaining under the lease. The landlord cannot claim the arrears from the guarantor. ☐

Flag for review

The claimant issues proceedings against the defendant for breach of contract arising from the installation of a heating system in their flower shop. The claimant claims that, due to inherent defects within the system, the heating failed to come on at the appropriate temperature on the night of 23 November. As a consequence, the claimant's entire stock of valuable roses died, causing losses of £43,000 and damage to their reputation in the industry. This is disputed by the defendant who submits that the fault lay with the claimant in their operation of the system. Both parties have instructed experts. The claimant is a multinational company whereas the defendant is an individual.

Which of the following best describes the approach the court would take when managing the claim?

A. The aim of the court is to deal with the case justly and at reasonable cost. As a consequence, the court will direct that a single joint expert be appointed to deal with liability.

B. The aim of the court is to deal with the case justly and at reasonable cost. As the amount in dispute is only £43,000, the court is unlikely to direct that a single joint expert be appointed.

C. The court will concentrate entirely on the merits of the case and will have no regard for the difference in status and financial position of the claimant and the defendant.

D. The court will take account of the fact this is a complex breach of contract claim requiring expert evidence and the level of damages sought is £43,000.

E. The court will allocate all the resources the claimant requires to resolve the matter because of the importance of the matter to the claimant.

Flag for review

The defendant is involved in a personal injury claim against them. It is alleged that the defendant negligently drove their car into the claimant, another road user, causing injury to the claimant. During the course of proceedings, a witness produces a witness statement recounting their version of events in the lead-up to the defendant driving home from a local pub. The witness was present at the pub from when the defendant arrived to when they left; the witness was sitting at the table next to the defendant the whole time. When describing the defendant's state of intoxication, the witness states that the defendant had drunk 'nine pints of beer' and was 'too drunk to drive a car'.

Which of the following statements most accurately sets out the status of the firm's professional indemnity for the 30 days following the expiration of the indemnity insurance policy?

A. The evidence of how many pints the defendant drank is admissible as direct evidence, but the evidence that the defendant was too drunk to drive a car is inadmissible as opinion evidence.

B. Both the evidence of how many pints the defendant drank and that the defendant was too drunk to drive a car are inadmissible as opinion evidence.

C. The evidence of how many pints the defendant drank is inadmissible as direct evidence, but the evidence that the defendant was too drunk to drive a car is admissible as opinion evidence.

D. Both the evidence of how many pints the defendant drank and that the defendant was too drunk to drive a car are admissible as opinion evidence.

E. The evidence of how many pints the defendant drank is admissible as opinion evidence, but the evidence that the defendant was too drunk to drive a car is inadmissible as opinion evidence.

Flag for review

A company brings a claim for breach of contract in the High Court, but is unsuccessful at trial. The company wishes to appeal to the Court of Appeal.

Which of the following best represents the basis upon which permission to appeal would be given?

A. The trial judge has incorrectly applied the law.

B. The trial judge has incorrectly interpreted the facts of the case.

C. The appeal would have a real prospect of success and there is some other compelling reason for the appeal to be heard.

D. The appeal would have a real prospect of success or there is some other compelling reason for the appeal to be heard.

E. The appeal would have more than a fanciful prospect of success and there is some other compelling reason for the appeal to be heard.

Flag for review

The claimant has successfully pursued a claim in private nuisance against a nightclub owner in a residential area close to their property. The nightclub owner obtained planning permission from the planning authority to develop the venue as a nightclub. The claimant wants the court to award an injunction to prevent the club from opening. The nightclub incorporates a restaurant and corporate venue, and employs 50 members of staff.

Which of the following will the court take into consideration when considering the granting of the injunction?

A. Whether the nightclub owner has caused the nuisance by way of negligence.

B. Whether the claimant has behaved reasonably in requesting the injunction.

C. Whether the nightclub is an unreasonable interference to the claimant's right of enjoyment.

D. Whether the presence of the nightclub signifies a disturbance to a class of people.

E. Whether a sum of money will adequately compensate the claimant.

Session 2 questions

Q57 of 90   Flag for review

The court is asked to assess the validity of a contract with a man who claims to have suffered from mental incapacity at the time the contract was formed.

When assessing the validity of the contract, which of the following best explains the effect of any mental incapacity?

A. The contract will be void once the court is satisfied that the man did not have mental capacity at the time of entering into the contract.

B. The contract will only be enforceable if the other party had taken reasonable steps to disprove any claim of capacity at the time the contract was made.

C. The contract will be set aside whenever there is evidence of mental incapacity.

D. The contract will be voidable if the man is able to prove he lacked mental capacity at the time of the contract, and that the other party knew or ought to have known about the incapacity.

E. The contract will be enforceable if the other party can prove that they did not know about any mental incapacity.

Q58 of 90   Flag for review

A solicitor agrees to act for a client on a 'no win, no fee' conditional fee agreement. The success fee is set at 25%. The solicitor's usual charging rate is £190 per hour. The work undertaken amounts to 20 hours of work. The client's claim is successful, and the client is awarded £4,000 in damages.

What success fee will the client be liable to pay?

A. A sum of £1,000.

B. A sum of £1,900.

C. A sum of £950.

D. A sum of £4,750.

E. The client is not liable to pay a success fee.

Flag for review ⚑

The Court of Justice of the European Union (CJEU) has recently decided a case that concerned the interpretation and application of a law that is part of EU retained law. In England, the Supreme Court is due to consider a case that concerns the interpretation and application of the same law.

To what extent is the decision of the CJEU binding on the Supreme Court?

A. The Supreme Court may choose to consider the CJEU decision but is not bound to follow it. ☐

B. The CJEU decision is binding on the Supreme Court because the case involves the interpretation and application of EU law. ☐

C. The decision is not binding on the Supreme Court because the decisions of the CJEU no longer have any effect on domestic law. ☐

D. The Supreme Court must consider and apply the decision of the CJEU because the issue concerns retained EU law. ☐

E. The Supreme Court is no longer permitted to consider or apply decisions of the CJEU to English law. ☐

Flag for review ⚑

A clause in a partnership agreement states as follows:

'7. DRAWINGS AND SALARIES

7.1 The Net Profits or Net Losses of the Partnership shall be divided equally between the Partners.

7.2 Each Partner shall be entitled to draw out of the Partnership Bank account for his own use, such sum as may from time to time be agreed by all the Partners on account of his drawings being his or her accruing share of the Net Profits for each Accounting Period provided that no sum shall be so drawn unless there is money in the account available for such purpose in excess of the monies necessary for the current expenses of the Partnership.

7.3 If in any Accounting Period the aggregate amount drawn out by any Partner shall be found to exceed the amount of his share of the Net Profits for that Accounting Period he shall repay within 30 days of the end of such Accounting Period such excess.

7.4 It is agreed that an annual salary in the sum of £30,000 shall be paid to the Partners and that this shall be in addition to such Partners' share of Net Profits and will not be on account of the same and furthermore that such salaries shall be paid whether or not there is sufficient cleared money in the Partnership Bank account available for such purpose. Such salaries shall be subject to increases as may from time to time be agreed by all the Partners.'

Which of the following statements best represents a combination of elements that exist in this partnership that deviate from the provisions of the Partnership Act 1890?

A. Apportionment of Net Profits/Losses, ability to make drawings and payment of a salary to each Partner. ☐

B. Apportionment of Net Profits/Losses, ability to make drawings, requirement to repay in the event of drawings exceeding a Partner's share of Net Profits and payment of a salary to each Partner. ☐

C. Ability to make drawings, requirement to repay in the event of drawings exceeding a Partner's share of Net Profits and payment of a salary to each Partner. ☐

D. Ability to make drawings and requirement to repay in the event of drawings exceeding a Partner's share of Net Profits. ☐

E. Apportionment of Net Profits/Losses, ability to make drawings and requirement to repay in the event of drawings exceeding a Partner's share of Net Profits. ☐

Q61 of 90

Flag for review

A man writes a letter to a woman offering to sell her his gold watch for £5,000. The man promises to keep his offer open for five days. The woman receives the letter two days later and immediately replies by Royal Mail accepting the man's offer. The woman's letter of acceptance is delayed in the postal system and finally arrives seven days after the man's initial offer was sent. In the meantime, six days after the man's offer was made, the man sells the watch to a third party. The woman has discovered that the watch has been sold and now brings a claim for breach of contract.

Which of the following statements best explains whether the man has breached his contract with the woman?

A. The man is not in breach of contract as his promise to keep the offer open for five days was not supported by consideration.

B. The man is in breach of contract as his promise to keep the offer open for five days was legally binding.

C. The man is not in breach of contract as the woman's letter of acceptance was received after the offer had lapsed.

D. The man is in breach of contract as the woman's letter of acceptance was effective when posted two days after receipt of the offer and before the watch was sold to a third party.

E. The man is not in breach of contract as the woman's acceptance was not communicated to the man before the offer had lapsed.

Q62 of 90

Flag for review

The claimant is a teacher at a local school that is undergoing renovation works. The contractors are working on the school during the summer holidays when there are no children on the premises. The claimant visits the school to collect some marking to complete over the holidays. They visit at lunchtime when most of the contractors are off-site. As the claimant walks into the school office, they trip over a toolbox, breaking their wrist and causing bruising to their face and body. The teacher brings a claim against the school.

What is the likely outcome of the claim?

A. The teacher's claim will likely fail against the school as the school was not responsible for the teacher's accident.

B. The teacher's claim will likely succeed against the school as the school has a non-delegable duty of care towards the health and safety of the teacher.

C. The teacher's claim will likely fail against the school as the teacher took the risk by attending the school during the period when they knew renovation works were taking place.

D. The teacher's claim will likely succeed against the school, but damages will be reduced to reflect the contributory negligence of the teacher.

E. The teacher's claim will likely fail against the school as the school cannot be expected to know the claimant would attend the school premises.

Flag for review 🏳

A solicitor represents a client in civil proceedings. The client has identified a witness that will support their version of events. The client has identified that the witness will not give evidence unless they are paid for acting as a witness.

How should the solicitor act in response to the request for payment?

A. The solicitor can offer to pay the witness to give evidence on behalf of the client. ☐

B. The solicitor can only offer to pay the witness to give evidence on behalf of the client if the court consents to it. ☐

C. The solicitor cannot offer to pay the witness to give evidence on behalf of the client, including expenses for attending court. ☐

D. The solicitor can only offer to pay the witness for their expenses of attending court to give evidence on behalf of the client. ☐

E. The solicitor cannot offer to pay the witness to give evidence on behalf of the client unless the witness gives a statement that they would not otherwise give evidence. ☐

Flag for review 🏳

The claimant's brother is involved in a serious train crash in which over 50 people are killed. The claimant's brother is taken by the emergency services to the hospital but dies on the way to the hospital. The claimant has not seen their brother for over 30 years but, as the only surviving member of the family, is requested to identify the brother's body at the hospital morgue. The brother's face and body are significantly burnt and disfigured. The claimant arrives minutes after the brother is pronounced dead. Upon seeing their brother's body, the claimant suffers a severe stress reaction which is later diagnosed as post-traumatic stress disorder (PTSD).

Which of the following best describes the difficulties that the claimant may face in bringing a claim for psychiatric harm?

A. The claimant did not suffer a medically diagnosed psychiatric illness. ☐

B. The claimant did not witness the immediate aftermath of the incident. ☐

C. The claimant did not have a close tie of love and affection with their brother. ☐

D. The claimant was not in the zone of danger. ☐

E. The claimant is not the brother's next of kin. ☐

Q65 of 90   Flag for review 🏳

A solicitor represents the claimant in a personal injury dispute. The solicitor's firm receives documentation intended for the defence by mistake. The solicitor has not yet read the papers, having discovered the error immediately upon opening the communication.

Which of the following best describes what the solicitor should do in the circumstances?

A. The solicitor is obliged to read the papers and make the claimant aware of all information contained in those papers material to the manner in question.

B. The solicitor is obliged to return the papers unread to the defendant's solicitors but must inform the claimant that they received the papers in error.

C. The solicitor is obliged to make the claimant aware that they have received the papers in error and seek the claimant's instructions on how to proceed.

D. The solicitor is obliged to read the papers but is not required to make the claimant aware of all information contained in those papers material to the manner in question.

E. The solicitor is obliged to return the papers unread to the defendant's solicitors and is not required to inform the claimant that they received the papers in error.

Q66 of 90   Flag for review 🏳

A solicitor is instructed by a client who is the defendant in a criminal matter. The defendant is charged with a serious indictable-only offence. The defendant insists that she is not guilty of the offence. The defendant is a teacher and would most likely lose their job if convicted of the offence.

Which of the following best describes the client's eligibility for legal aid in respect of this matter?

A. The client may be eligible for legal aid if they can show that they are likely to lose their liberty as a result of the proceedings.

B. The client is eligible for legal aid because they are charged with an indictable-only offence and may receive a custodial sentence.

C. The client may be eligible for legal aid if they are able to demonstrate they have a reasonable chance of proving their innocence.

D. The client would automatically meet the interest of justice test but would only be eligible for legal aid if they met the relevant eligibility requirements in respect of the means test.

E. The client may be eligible for legal aid if they can pass the interest of justice test and the means test.

Q67 of 90

Flag for review

The owners of a local theme park are aware that children try to access the park at night. The owners have installed cameras to catch them and increased the level of security around the park. Two 11-year-old children force open and climb through a gap in the fence surrounding the theme park. This is captured on security cameras and a guard is despatched to find the children. The two children climb up a rollercoaster but slip and fall. One child dies and the other is left with life-changing injuries. Both children's parents bring claims for personal injury under the Occupiers' Liability Act 1984 against the theme park owners.

Which of the following best describes the likely outcome of the claims against the owners of the theme park?

A. The claims will likely succeed on the basis that the theme park owners knew children were entering the park at night.

B. The claims will likely fail on the basis that a reasonable person would not have entered the premises at night.

C. The claims will likely succeed on the basis that the theme park owners owe a special duty of care to children.

D. The claims will likely fail on the basis that the injuries were not caused by the state of the premises.

E. The claims will likely succeed but damages will be reduced significantly due to the childrens' contributory negligence.

Q68 of 90

Flag for review

Company A and Company B are haulage companies, and both own a number of commercial vehicles.

Which of the following statements represents a transaction that would require shareholder approval as a substantial property transaction?

A. The purchase of a commercial vehicle owned by Company A by a director of Company A when the director is paying the market value of £4,500 for the vehicle.

B. The purchase of a commercial vehicle owned by Company B by an employee of Company B when the employee is paying the market value of £4,500 for the vehicle.

C. The purchase of a fleet of commercial vehicles owned by Company A by an employee of Company A when the employee is paying the market value of £104,500 for the vehicles.

D. The purchase of a fleet of commercial vehicles owned by Company B by the father of a director of Company B when the buyer is paying the market value of £104,500 for the vehicles.

E. The purchase of a fleet of commercial vehicles by Company A from the father of a director of Company A when the seller is receiving shares in Company A worth approximately £120,000 in exchange for the vehicles.

Q69 of 90   Flag for review

A man purchased a brand-new television from a retailer. The television was found to be defective and the man sought a refund from the retailer. The retailer refused to issue a refund. The retailer stated that the television was defective due to the fault of the manufacturer. The man now seeks to bring a claim for breach of contract against the manufacturer.

Which of the following best explains whether the man can bring a claim against the manufacturer for breach of contract?

A. The man can bring a claim against the manufacturer, as the manufacturer is strictly liable for the defective product.

B. The man cannot bring a claim against the manufacturer as the man must first give the retailer the opportunity to repair the television.

C. The doctrine of privity of contract prevents the man from bringing a claim against the manufacturer.

D. The man can bring a claim against the manufacturer, as the manufacturer has been negligent in the production of the television.

E. The man cannot bring a claim against the manufacturer, as the manufacturer does not owe a duty of care to users of the products.

Q70 of 90   Flag for review

The claimant is a burglar who forced entry to the defendant's house and was attacked by the defendant's dog. There is a sign on the exterior of the defendant's house that alerts visitors to the presence of the dog. The claimant brings a claim against the defendant for personal injury and loss of earnings. As a result of the dog bites, the claimant required skin grafts and an extended stay in hospital during which they were unable to work as a delivery driver.

Which of the following best describes how the defendant should defend the claim made by the claimant?

A. The defendant should defend the claim on the basis that the claimant consented to being bitten by the dog when they broke into the defendant's house.

B. The defendant should allow their home insurers to pay the claim on the basis that they owed the claimant a duty of care.

C. The defendant should pay the claim but seek a reduction for contributory negligence on the basis the claimant should have heeded the sign about the dog.

D. The defendant should defend the claim on the basis that the claimant was involved in a criminal enterprise and should not be able to claim for injury.

E. The defendant should admit liability but dispute the value of the claim for lost earnings.

Flag for review 🏳

The claimant is an ice-skating coach and is injured in an accident at work which leaves them with loss of feeling and sensation in their right leg. The claimant's employer admits liability for the accident and is due to pay the claimant an amount by way of compensation. The claimant is unable to work as an ice-skating coach, but their employer offers them a role as a receptionist. Whilst working as a receptionist, a member of the public assaults the claimant, leaving them with a broken nose. The claimant wishes to bring a second claim against their employer, in addition to their original claim, on the basis that had they been working as an ice-skating coach, the assault would not have happened.

Is the second claim likely to succeed?

A.   Yes: but for the employer's initial negligence, the claimant would not be working on reception and be injured when the member of the public became aggressive.

B.   No: the assault is a new intervening act that breaks the chain of causation.

C.   Yes: the assault is a direct consequence of the employer's negligence.

D.   No: the employer has the defence of consent as the claimant consented to changing jobs following their accident.

E.   Yes: the claimant's injuries are a foreseeable risk associated with their initial injury.

Flag for review 🏳

A firm has recently employed a new trainee solicitor. The trainee solicitor is a Muslim woman who wears a hijab as part of her religious beliefs. The trainee solicitor has been informed by a senior partner that there is a strict dress code at the law firm, and head coverings are not permissible. The trainee solicitor has expressed her concerns regarding the dress code to her supervisor.

Which of the following best describes the course of conduct the supervisor should take?

A.   The supervisor should advise the trainee solicitor to comply with the dress code and remove her hijab.

B   The supervisor should explain to the trainee solicitor that the dress code is religiously and culturally neutral and must be followed by all employees.

C   The supervisor should suggest that the trainee solicitor speak to the senior partner and explain the significance of the hijab to her religious beliefs.

D   The supervisor should offer to speak to the senior partner on behalf of the trainee solicitor and seek a reasonable adjustment to the dress code.

E   The supervisor should advise the trainee solicitor that she has the right to wear the hijab in the workplace, and the firm is required to make a reasonable adjustment to the dress code.

Q73 of 90   Flag for review 🏳

The local museum hosts a fashion show. The museum ropes off the top floor, which houses a collection of contemporary toys. The fashion show takes place on the first floor. Tickets are issued, which state the fashion show is for individuals over the age of 18 only. One of the attendees attends with their three-year-old child without the knowledge of the security team. During the fashion show, the three-year-old child visits the top floor unsupervised by their attendee parent where they play with some of the toys on display. The three-year-old child makes their way back to the first floor and in doing so falls down a flight of stairs and is seriously injured.

What is the likely view of the court relating to the museum's negligence?

A. The court is likely to find the museum negligent on the basis that they have created an allurement with the contemporary toys on display.

B. The court is unlikely to find the museum negligent on the basis that the three-year-old child should not have attended the event and should have been supervised by their attendee parent.

C. The court is likely to find the museum negligent on the basis that they have failed to ensure that visitors are reasonably safe.

D. The court is unlikely to find the museum negligent on the basis that the three-year-old child was a trespasser and the museum does not owe the child a duty of care.

E. The court is likely to find the museum negligent on the basis that but for their negligence, the three-year-old child would not have been injured.

Q74 of 90   Flag for review 🏳

The Supreme Court has recently issued a declaration of incompatibility under section 4 of the Human Rights Act 1998. As a result of the ruling, a draft remedial order has been presented to Parliament.

Which of the following statements best describes the nature of remedial orders?

A. A remedial order is a type of remedy that is available where a court has issued a declaration of incompatibility under section 4 of the Human Rights Act 1998.

B. A remedial order is a type of statutory instrument that allows the Government to quickly amend Acts of Parliament so as to remove incompatibility with the Human Rights Act 1998.

C. A remedial order is a type of statutory instrument that allows Parliament to quickly overturn legislation deemed to be incompatible with the Human Rights Act 1998.

D. A remedial order is a type of bill that must pass through the usual legislative process before it can become law. This type of bill is used to remedy incompatibility with the Human Rights Act 1998.

E. A remedial order is a direction to Parliament to amend Acts of Parliament so as to remove incompatibility with the Human Rights Act 1998.

Flag for review ⚑

The Court of Appeal (Civil Division) is considering a complex contract law appeal. During the course of the appeal, various questions have arisen as to the precise meaning of a phrase contained within a statute. Both parties have put forward submissions regarding the correct interpretation of the phrase. A leading and highly respected academic in the field of contract law has explored the relevant section of the statute extensively and has published articles on the matter. The judges hearing the appeal feel it would be useful to refer to the relevant articles to assist them in construing the relevant section of the statute.

Which of the following statements most accurately describes the extent to which the Court of Appeal (Civil Division) can use such external aids to assist in interpreting the statute?

A. The Court of Appeal (Civil Division) may refer to external aids such as academic writings as the statute is unclear. In this case, the Court may refer to the academic articles to assist them in interpreting the relevant legislation. ☐

B. The Court of Appeal (Civil Division) may refer to external aids such as academic writings if it wishes to. In this case, the Court may refer to the academic writings to assist them in interpreting the relevant legislation. ☐

C. The Court of Appeal (Civil Division) may refer to external aids such as academic writings if both parties agree and the Court feels it would assist in interpreting the relevant provision. ☐

D. The Court of Appeal (Civil Division) may not refer to academic writings since they are not parliamentary publications. ☐

E. The Court of Appeal (Civil Division) may refer to external aids as the statute is unclear. However, academic writings are not recognised as external aids to statutory interpretation. ☐

Flag for review ⚑

A company approaches a solicitor for advice on the appointment of a new director. The solicitor advises that there are a number of ways in which this can be achieved.

Which of the following statements would not be suitable advice for the company as it would not result in a valid and effective appointment of a director?

A. The company should pass a board resolution to appoint and notify Companies House of the appointment. ☐

B. The company should pass a board resolution to call an extraordinary general meeting, an ordinary resolution to appoint, and notify Companies House of the appointment. ☐

C. The company should pass a board resolution to appoint and award a fixed-term service contract for one year, keeping a copy of the service contract at the Registered Office, and notify Companies House of the appointment. ☐

D. The company should pass a board resolution to call an extraordinary general meeting, an ordinary resolution to appoint, awarding of a rolling contract of employment (terminable upon three months' notice by either side) by the board, keeping a copy of the contract at the Registered Office, and notify Companies House of the appointment. ☐

E. The company should award a rolling contract of employment (terminable upon three months' notice by either side) by the board, keeping a copy of the contract at the Registered Office, and notify Companies House of the appointment. ☐

A solicitor is instructed to act on behalf of a client in respect of a divorce. The client's case is straightforward as both parties to the marriage consent to a divorce and plan to make a joint application for a divorce order. The parties do not have children and have a marital property agreement in place to determine how the marital property will be distributed.

Which of the following is the most appropriate funding option in this case?

A. A conditional fee agreement.

B. A damages-based agreement.

C. After-the-event insurance.

D. A fixed-fee arrangement.

E. A private retainer.

An entrepreneur with a number of sources of income has a taxable income of £100,000. They are thinking of setting up a new business with another person where the profit projections are £90,000 in the first year. The entrepreneur is concerned about the amount of tax that would be payable on any profits.

Which of the following business types is the best option in light of the entrepreneur's concerns over tax liabilities?

A. A traditional partnership.

B. A limited liability partnership.

C. A private company limited by shares.

D. A joint venture between two sole traders.

E. A sole trader.

Flag for review

A newly qualified solicitor is instructed on a complex commercial contract case with a senior partner. The senior partner has tasked the newly qualified solicitor with drafting a key document for the case. However, the newly qualified solicitor has doubts about their competence in handling such a complex case. The senior partner has requested the document to be completed in a short period of time.

Which of the following best describes the newly qualified solicitor's obligations under the Solicitors Regulation Authority (SRA) Code of Conduct?

A. The newly qualified solicitor should decline to undertake the senior partner's task to draft the key document.

B. The newly qualified solicitor should undertake the senior partner's task to draft the key document.

C. The newly qualified solicitor should delegate the senior partner's task to draft the key document to a paralegal in the law firm who has expertise in complex commercial transactions.

D. The newly qualified solicitor should request an extension on the senior partner's task to draft the key document to give her the opportunity to gain the competence to complete the task.

E. The newly qualified solicitor should cease to act for the client.

Flag for review

A senior solicitor in a law firm makes a joke about a trainee solicitor's sexual orientation in front of other employees. The trainee solicitor finds the joke offensive and humiliating, and reports the incident to a managing partner.

Which of the following statements most accurately describes the senior partner's behaviour?

A. The behaviour would amount to direct discrimination on the basis of the trainee solicitor's sexual orientation and would contravene the Equality Act 2010.

B. The behaviour would amount to indirect discrimination on the basis of the trainee solicitor's sexual orientation and would contravene the Equality Act 2010.

C. The behaviour would amount to victimisation contrary to the Equality Act 2010.

D. The behaviour would amount to direct discrimination on the basis of the trainee solicitor's sexual orientation but would be considered to be justified under the Equality Act 2010.

E. The behaviour would amount to harassment contrary to the Equality Act 2010.

Q81 of 90   Flag for review 🏴

A defendant is defending proceedings brought against them for recovery of money which the claimant alleges they paid towards the restoration of the claimant's classic car. The defendant denies that any money was paid by the claimant to anybody in connection with the restoration project. The court orders that the parties undertake disclosure on the standard basis. Whilst looking through records, the defendant finds a receipt from their garage, which shows a payment was received from the claimant in cash for rebuilding the engine to that classic car.

Which of the following best represents the position concerning disclosure?

A. The defendant does not need to disclose this document as it is adverse to their defence.

B. The defendant does need to disclose the document as they are under a duty to disclose any document that is relevant to the claim. Failing to do so would leave the defendant in breach of the order.

C. The defendant does not need to disclose this document as it is for the claimant to disclose evidence that supports their claim.

D. The defendant does need to disclose the document as they have previously denied that any money was paid. Failing to do so would leave the defendant in breach of the order.

E. The defendant does not need to disclose this document as they have not been specifically directed to do so by the court.

Q82 of 90   Flag for review 🏴

A music promoter entered into a contract to hire a concert hall owned by the local council. Two days before the date of hire, the concert hall was destroyed by fire. The fire was the fault of neither party.

Which of the following statements best explains the legal position?

A. The local council is in breach of the contract if the hire cannot take place, due to the doctrine of absolute obligations.

B. The local council is in breach of the contract, as they should have taken reasonable steps to avoid the fire.

C. The local council will be discharged of any future obligations under the contract as the contract is frustrated.

D. The local council and the music promoter will be discharged of all obligations under the contract as the contract is frustrated.

E. The music promoter will be able to claim damages to recover the loss of profit they would have made had the contract not been breached.

Flag for review 🏳

The claimant is a front-seat passenger in the defendant's vehicle when the defendant drives into the rear of another vehicle at a roundabout. The claimant is not wearing a seatbelt. The medical evidence shows that the claimant's failure to wear a seatbelt had no impact on the claimant's injuries.

What is the likely outcome of the claim against the defendant?

A. The claim will likely fail on the basis the claimant failed to wear a seatbelt.

B. The claim will likely succeed but damages will be reduced by 25% to reflect contributory negligence.

C. The claim will likely succeed but damages will be reduced by 15% to reflect contributory negligence.

D. The claim will likely fail as there has been a break in the chain of causation.

E. The claim will likely succeed and there will be no reduction for contributory negligence.

Flag for review 🏳

A claimant is in the final stages of a claim against a defendant over an alleged breach of contract, with damages claimed valued at £84,000. The defendant writes to the claimant with a list of documents that they require to be included in the trial bundle. The claimant believes that the amount of documentation that the defendant is asking to be included is unreasonable and would take them a disproportionate amount of time to reproduce as part of the bundle.

Which of the following best represents what the claimant should do?

A. The claimant must agree the contents of the trial bundle with the defendant and deal with the preparation of the bundle, including making sufficient copies for the court, all parties and all witnesses. The trial bundle must contain all documents upon which all parties are intending to rely in the trial.

B. The claimant should write back to the defendant and advise that, if they wish to include the volume of documents as indicated, they must prepare the trial bundle themselves. The claimant should enclose copies of all documents upon which they intend to rely at trial to enable the defendant to prepare the trial bundle.

C. The claimant should write back to the defendant and advise them to prepare their own trial bundle which should be filed on the same date as that of the claimant.

D. The claimant should write back to the defendant and advise them that they will only include the number of documents that are proportionate to the value of the claim in the trial bundle.

E. The claimant should make an emergency application to the court for an order specifying which of the defendant's documents should form part of the trial bundle.

Q85 of 90   Flag for review 🏴

A major law firm recently dealt with a high-value property transaction. The solicitors managing the client's file had concerns about money laundering, which they duly reported to the firm's nominated officer.

Which of the following statements most accurately describes the steps that the nominated officer should have taken following the disclosure?

A. The nominated officer should have made a disclosure to the Solicitors Regulation Authority as soon as is practicable. ☐

B. The nominated officer should have made a Suspicious Activity Report to the National Crime Agency as soon as practicable. ☐

C. The nominated officer should have made a Suspicious Activity Report to the Solicitors Regulation Authority as soon as practicable. ☐

D. The nominated officer should have made a disclosure to the Financial Action Task Force Authority as soon as practicable. ☐

E. The nominated officer should have made a Suspicious Activity Report to the Financial Action Task Force Authority as soon as practicable. ☐

Q86 of 90   Flag for review 🏴

A client is a private company limited by shares that is operating successfully. The board of directors is considering declaring a dividend.

Which of the following statements represents the best advice on the use of dividends for the client?

A. Dividends may be declared by the board of directors if the client has made a profit once it has paid its corporation tax liability to HMRC. ☐

B. Dividends may be declared by the board of directors if the client has made a profit. ☐

C. Dividends must be declared by the board of directors if the client has made a profit once it has paid its corporation tax liability to HMRC. ☐

D. Dividends may be declared by the board of directors and are treated as a deductible expense of the business when calculating the client's profits. ☐

E. Dividends may be declared by the board of directors and it is the client's responsibility to pay the equivalent of the recipients' liability to income tax at the basic rate (but not the higher rate if applicable) to HMRC. ☐

Flag for review 🏳

A solicitor is acting on behalf of a client who claims they are the victim of a human rights violation. The solicitor discovers that the relevant statutory provision came into effect several years before the Human Rights Act 1998 was enacted.

Which of the following statements best describes the court's duty to interpret the legislation in a way that is compatible with the Human Rights Act 1998 and the European Convention on Human Rights?

A. Section 3 of the Human Rights Act 1998 requires courts to interpret primary and subordinate legislation in a way that is compatible with the Convention rights. However, this duty does not apply to legislation that was enacted before the Human Rights Act 1998 came into effect. ☐

B. Section 2 of the Human Rights Act 1998 requires courts so far as it is possible to do so to interpret primary and subordinate legislation in a way that is compatible with the Convention rights. ☐

C. Section 2 of the Human Rights Act 1998 requires courts to interpret primary and subordinate legislation in a way that is compatible with the Convention rights. However, this duty does not apply to legislation that was enacted before the Human Rights Act 1998 came into effect. ☐

D. Section 3 of the Human Rights Act 1998 requires courts so far as it is possible to do so to interpret primary and subordinate legislation in a way that is compatible with the Convention rights. ☐

E. Courts must follow the usual rules of statutory interpretation and ensure that, wherever possible, words are given their natural and literal meaning. ☐

Flag for review 🏳

Parliament has recently passed legislation that criminalises the sale and distribution of a new and dangerous drug.

Which of the following statements most accurately describes the presumptions that a court would presume are implied in the statute?

A. The court would presume that the statute does not apply retrospectively and that any criminal offences stated in the statute require proof of intention. ☐

B. The court would presume that the statute does not apply retrospectively, and that any criminal offences require proof of intention unless the statute expressly states otherwise. ☐

C. The court would presume that the statute does not apply retrospectively and comes into force on the stated commencement date. ☐

D. The court would presume that any criminal offences stated in the statute require proof of intention unless the statute implies otherwise. ☐

E. The court would presume that the statute alters any relevant pre-existing common law. ☐

Q89 of 90   Flag for review

A client company wishes to expand its business and has the opportunity of acquiring a competitor company. The client company needs to raise finance in order to achieve this but the existing shareholders do not want their current levels of control to be diluted.

Which of the following describes the option that is least likely to dilute the control of existing shareholders?

A.   An issue of preference shares to an outside private investor.

B.   A debenture including a fixed charge in favour of a high-street lender.

C.   An issue of ordinary shares to an outside private investor.

D.   An issue of ordinary shares to an existing shareholder.

E.   Sale of the entire share capital of the company to an interested buyer.

Q90 of 90   Flag for review

A client instructs a solicitor in respect of a personal injury matter. The solicitor and client meet to discuss the matter and explore the funding options that are available to the client. The solicitor advises the client that the case has good prospects of success (in excess of 60%). The client informs the solicitor that they intend to pay their legal costs by use of cover provided through a travel insurance policy and, if necessary, pay any additional costs from their own funds.

Which of the following statements most accurately describes the sources of funding in this matter?

A.   The client will fund the case through a before-the-event insurance policy only.

B.   The client will fund the case through an after-the-event insurance policy and a private retainer.

C.   The client will fund the case through an after-the-event insurance policy only.

D.   The client will fund the case through a before-the-event insurance and a private retainer.

E.   The client will pay her legal costs through a private retainer only.

◼ REFLECTION

CANDIDATE INSTRUCTIONS

Session 2, and the test, has now ended. In the real SQE1 assessment, once Session 2 has ended you cannot return to this session, nor can you return to Session 1.

In the real assessment, you will see a display screen that reminds you about how to access your results. This information has been summarised on **page 153**. Please also note the timings on the SQE section of the SRA's website for the release of results.

PAUSE TO REFLECT

Now that you have completed the *Prepare for SQE1: FLK1 Practice Assessment*, reflect on your experience. Be honest with yourself in considering the reflective questions in Table 4.

Table 4: Reflecting on your FLK1 practice assessment

How did it feel to take a closed-book timed assessment?	• Did you feel prepared to sit the simulated SQE1-style assessment? • Did you feel confident in your ability to answer the questions without any resources to assist you?
How did you feel about sitting the assessment in general?	• Have you got experience of sitting these types of assessments? • If not, how can you ensure that you are physically and mentally prepared to sit them?
Did you feel under pressure because of the time limit?	• Is there anything you can do to assist in this pressure? • Do you need to review your approach to answering MCQs?
Did you answer the MCQs in the time period permitted?	• If not, do you appreciate that in the real assessment, you will not have the opportunity to revisit any MCQs that you failed to answer? • Do you need to review your style/approach to answering MCQs?
Did you answer the MCQs without using any resources (other than a permitted calculator)?	• If not, do you need to revise the content for FLK1 more thoroughly? • Do you need more time to prepare for the assessment? • What more do you need to do to prepare yourself?

Now, ask yourself one final question: **Are you ready for FLK1?**

YES ☐ NO ☐

RESULTS AND ANSWERS

You will find the answers to *Prepare for SQE1: FLK1 Practice Assessment* overleaf.

Please note that you will not be provided with the answers or your results at the end of your SQE1 assessment. In the real assessment, you will receive your results approximately 5–6 weeks after sitting SQE1. The actual date of your results will be confirmed closer to your assessment. Further details are available on **page 153**.

For this practice assessment, you can use the Answer section as an opportunity to review your knowledge and understanding. Our advice is to review the answer in full and tick the box to record whether or not you chose the correct answer.

Session 1 answers

■ SUMMARY

The following table is a quick reference guide for the answers to Session 1 of *Prepare for SQE1: FLK1 Practice Assessment*. Consider using a coloured pen or a highlighter to mark the MCQs that you answered correctly and score yourself 1 mark for each. Add up your total marks, and calculate your percentage for Session 1.

For a summary of the Session 2 answers, see **page 122**.

Question	Answer	Question	Answer	Question	Answer
1	D	31	D	61	D
2	B	32	B	62	B
3	E	33	A	63	C
4	E	34	A	64	C
5	A	35	E	65	E
6	B	36	E	66	D
7	D	37	D	67	B
8	B	38	C	68	A
9	A	39	A	69	E
10	A	40	B	70	D
11	D	41	A	71	A
12	B	42	D	72	B
13	D	43	C	73	B
14	C	44	C	74	B
15	C	45	E	75	D
16	E	46	B	76	C
17	A	47	D	77	C
18	D	48	A	78	D
19	D	49	A	79	C
20	C	50	A	80	B
21	D	51	C	81	D
22	E	52	A	82	C
23	B	53	E	83	C
24	A	54	E	84	A
25	A	55	A	85	D
26	E	56	C	86	C
27	D	57	E	87	B
28	B	58	E	88	A
29	C	59	D	89	C
30	B	60	A	90	C

Your total score for Session 1: _____ / 90

Percentage: _____ %

■ DETAILED ANSWERS

A1 of 90 (page 1)   **Area of law assessed: Dispute resolution**

The correct answer was D. This is because the court would a most certainly impose a costs sanction, due to the client refusing the opponent's attempts to mediate, by ordering them to pay their own legal costs and fees as well as a percentage of the client's. Options A and B are incorrect as it is unlikely that the allegations of non-performance would have any bearing on the court's decision relating to costs and, given the refusal to mediate, it is unlikely the court would adopt a 'costs follow the event approach' here. Option C is not correct as it is very unlikely that the court would order the client to pay full costs for a single refusal to mediate. Option E is not correct as it is unlikely that the opponent would be penalised, given they made the offer to mediate in the first place.

Did you choose the correct answer?   YES ☐   NO ☐

See *Revise SQE: Dispute Resolution*, **Chapter 1** for a discussion of this area of law.

A2 of 90 (page 2)   **Area of law assessed: Contract law**

The correct answer was B. This is because consideration must be legally sufficient, but does not need to be adequate. The payment of £2,000 and the promise to pay the remaining amount the next day will be legally sufficient as consideration. The woman is therefore bound by her promise to sell the car to the man and will be in breach of contract if she refuses sale, or if she were to sell the car to the third party in the meantime. Option A is incorrect as it is irrelevant that the third party has offered more overall. The man has already formed an agreement with the woman and has provided sufficient consideration. The woman is obliged to sell the car to the man. Option C is incorrect because the payment of £2,000 and the promise to pay the remainder will be sufficient consideration. It is irrelevant that it is less than the market value. The court is not concerned with the adequacy of the consideration, or whether it is a good deal for the woman. Generally, there is no obligation to keep an offer open for a specified time. However, the woman has given her promise to sell in exchange for the man's promise to pay and the payment of the deposit. The woman has formed a binding agreement with the man, which is supported by consideration (therefore option D is incorrect). Option E is incorrect as the payment of the £2,000 deposit and the promise to pay the remainder are given in exchange for the woman's promise to sell. This is sufficient consideration.

Did you choose the correct answer?   YES ☐   NO ☐

See *Revise SQE: Contract Law*, **Chapter 2** for a discussion of this area of law.

A3 of 90 (page 2)   **Area of law assessed: Legal services**

The correct answer was E. This is because certain reserved legal activities may only be carried on by specified regulated legal service providers. Solicitors are a registered legal service provider and are subject to the regulation of the Solicitors Regulation Authority (SRA). The SRA may authorise solicitors to carry on reserved legal activities *except* notarial activities. Option A is incorrect because solicitors cannot carry on notarial activities. Option B is incorrect because a solicitor may exercise a right of audience. Option C is incorrect because it implies that freelance solicitors are unable to carry on reserved legal activities under any circumstances. Solicitors operating on a freelance basis may carry on all reserved legal activities except notarial activities, providing those activities are provided through an authorised body or the solicitor's organisation is registered as a recognised role practice (therefore option D is incorrect). Option E is therefore the most accurate description of the solicitor's authorisation to carry on reserved legal activities.

Did you choose the correct answer?   YES ☐   NO ☐

See *Revise SQE: The Legal System and Services of England and Wales*, **Chapter 5** for a discussion of this area of law.

A4 of 90 (page 3)   **Area of law assessed: Tort law**

The correct answer was E. This is because the accident was caused by the defendant's negligence, but the court will reduce the claimant's damages to reflect that the failure to wear a bicycle helmet has contributed to the claimant's injuries. Options A and B are incorrect as although the onus is on the reversing driver to ensure the road is clear and the cyclist does have the right of way, the court will find that the claimant's lack of a bicycle helmet has contributed to their injuries. Option C is incorrect as the claimant had the right of way and the defendant should have checked the road before reversing. Option D is incorrect as a party cannot be 100% contributorily negligent.

Did you choose the correct answer?   YES ☐   NO ☐

See *Revise SQE: Tort Law*, **Chapter 4** for a discussion of this area of law.

A5 of 90 (page 3)   **Area of law assessed: Dispute resolution**

The correct answer was A. This is because arbitration is the best option as it can be arranged relatively quickly and will guarantee a conclusion to the dispute, which will enable the building work to recommence and minimise the ongoing financial damage being caused to the client (therefore option B is incorrect). In this case, mediation is unlikely to be the best option for the parties, given how entrenched they are in their positions (options C and D are therefore incorrect). Option E is incorrect as litigation is also unlikely to be the best option as it is more likely to protract matters even further and increase overall costs.

Did you choose the correct answer?   YES ☐   NO ☐

See *Revise SQE: Dispute Resolution*, **Chapter 1** for a discussion of this area of law.

A6 of 90 (page 4)   **Area of law assessed: Tort law**

The correct answer was B. This is because all road users owe a duty of care to each other. The court will conclude that a reasonable road user would have stopped the vehicle the instant they felt unwell on the basis they were being investigated for a health condition that had previously rendered them unconscious (therefore option D is incorrect). Options A and C are incorrect as the standard of care is that of a reasonable road user; there are no adjustments made for professional or impaired road users. Option E is incorrect as the accident was caused by the defendant's negligence in failing to stop the vehicle the instance they felt unwell, and this is not an unavoidable incident that could not have been prevented.

Did you choose the correct answer?   YES ☐   NO ☐

See *Revise SQE: Tort Law*, **Chapter 1** for a discussion of this area of law.

A7 of 90 (page 4)   **Area of law assessed: Business law and practice**

The correct answer was D. This is because the MCQ asks you which of the following does not represent an accurate statement of law. Option D is the only option that is incorrect in law; the timeframe required is 28 days and not 21 days as stated. The fourth director should receive notice (meaning option A is correct in law, but the wrong option). As the MCQ tells you that the company has amended the model articles of association but does not give you further information about th s, the solicitor must check the articles of association for any such clause (therefore option B is incorrect). Options C and E also reflect accurate statements of law.

Did you choose the correct answer?   YES ☐   NO ☐

See *Revise SQE: Business Law and Practice*, **Chapter 4** for a discussion of this area of law.

A8 of 90 (page 5)   Area of law assessed: Legal services

The correct answer was B. This is because there are a number of regulated legal service providers, and each provider is subject to the regulation of a different regulatory body. Costs lawyers are subject to the Costs Lawyer Standards Board. Costs lawyers are not subject to any other regulatory body, so Options A, C, D and E are all incorrect.

Did you choose the correct answer?   YES ☐   NO ☐

See *Revise SQE: The Legal System and Services of England and Wales*, **Chapter 5** for a discussion of this area of law.

A9 of 90 (page 5)   Area of law assessed: Business law and practice

The correct answer was A. This is because in order to hold a meeting at short notice, 90% of the shareholders must agree, and on the figures, this must be unanimous here. Option B is incorrect because the chairperson of an extraordinary general meeting does not get a casting vote. Option C is incorrect because a special resolution can only be blocked by more than 25% of the vote (shareholders B and D could block). Option D is incorrect because Model Article 14 does not apply to alleged conflicts of interest for shareholders. Option E is incorrect because any shareholder with 10% or more of the shares can request a poll vote.

Did you choose the correct answer?   YES ☐   NO ☐

See *Revise SQE: Business Law and Practice*, **Chapter 4** for a discussion of this area of law.

A10 of 90 (page 6)   Area of law assessed: Tort law

The correct answer was A. This is because a claimant (suffering from mesothelioma) can recover damages from all responsible persons in breach of duty concerning exposure to asbestos (whether by having materially increased the risk or for any other reason). The responsible person is both jointly and severally liable. Option B is incorrect as the responsible factory will be jointly and severally liable. Option C is incorrect as remoteness relates to legal causation. The question relates to factual causation. The factual cause of the claimant's condition is exposure to asbestos which occurred when she hugged her father as a child and her father was negligently exposed to asbestos. Option D is incorrect as contributory negligence relates to whether the claimant has contributed to her injuries, and she did not voluntarily accept the risk as she was a child. Option E is incorrect as a claimant (suffering from mesothelioma) can recover damages from all responsible persons in breach of duty concerning exposure to asbestos (whether by having materially increased the risk or for any other reason), the responsible person being both jointly and severally liable.

Did you choose the correct answer?   YES ☐   NO ☐

See *Revise SQE: Tort Law*, **Chapter 2** for a discussion of this area of law.

A11 of 90 (page 6)   Area of law assessed: Contract law

The correct answer was D. This is because as the contract is concluded upon dispatch of the coffee machine, the notice provided with the delivery, therefore, comes too late. Reasonable notice must be provided before or at the time the contract is formed. Even if the clause were incorporated into the contract (which it is not on the facts), this is not an accurate statement. The law on unfair contract terms provides that a seller can exclude such liability, but only so far as the clause is reasonable (therefore option A is incorrect). Option B is incorrect as, although limited bargaining position is relevant to the assessment of whether a clause is unfair, on this occasion the notice is too late to be incorporated into the contract. Option C is incorrect because reasonable notice has not been provided before or at the time the contract was formed. The contract was completed on dispatch of the coffee machine. The notice on the document included with the delivery comes too late. Even if the clause were incorporated (which it is not on the facts), there is no evidence of liability in negligence. The liability is strict. The claim arises in breach of contract, and such liability seems to be clearly covered by the wording of the clause (therefore option E is incorrect).

Did you choose the correct answer?   YES ☐   NO ☐

See *Revise SQE: Contract Law*, **Chapter 6** for a discussion of this area of law.

A12 of 90 (page 7)   Area of law assessed: Dispute resolution

The correct answer was B. This is because whilst the pre-action protocol is important, the court will not penalise a party for failure to comply with it if this impacts on issuing proceedings within the relevant limitation period (therefore options C and D are incorrect). However, if proceedings are issued without complying with the pre-action protocol, requesting a stay will give the parties the ability to comply with all of their pre-action requirements without placing the limitation period at risk (therefore option A is incorrect). Option E is incorrect as having insufficient time to comply with the pre-action protocol is not a barrier to issuing proceedings.

Did you choose the correct answer?   YES ☐   NO ☐

See *Revise SQE: Dispute Resolution*, **Chapter 2** for a discussion of this area of law.

A13 of 90 (page 7)   Area of law assessed: Ethics and professional conduct

The correct answer was D. This is because the SRA Code of Conduct requires solicitors not to mislead or attempt to mislead their clients, the court or others, either by their own acts or omissions or allowing or being complicit in the acts or omissions of others (including their client). The solicitor would mislead the court and the claimant should the training log not be disclosed and the defendant continue to allege that the claimant was provided with a day-long training course (option B is therefore incorrect). If the defendant continues in his refusal to allow disclosure, the solicitor must withdraw from the case. Options A, C and E are incorrect as they would involve a breach of confidentiality; the solicitor is obliged to maintain the affairs of clients confidential.

Did you choose the correct answer?   YES ☐   NO ☐

See *Revise SQE: Ethics and Professional Conduct*, **Chapter 2** for a discussion of this area of law.

A14 of 90 (page 8)   Area of law assessed: Legal services

The correct answer was C. This is because a paralegal who is working within an SRA-regulated firm is subject to the SRA Code of Conduct (option B is therefore incorrect). It is essential that all solicitors and employees within SRA-regulated firms are aware of the contents of SRA Code of Conduct and understand their obligations under the Code. The fact that the paralegal is not a qualified/practising solicitor is irrelevant, so Options A and D are incorrect. The SRA Code of Conduct applies irrespective of whether the work they undertake constitutes reserved legal activities (therefore, Option E is incorrect).

Did you choose the correct answer?   YES ☐   NO ☐

See *Revise SQE: The Legal System and Services of England and Wales*, **Chapter 5** for a discussion of this area of law.

A15 of 90 (page 8)   Area of law assessed: Contract law

The correct answer was C. This is because advertisements are usually presumed to be invitations to treat, and not offers for sale. If the advertisement were an offer, then this would create a problem of multi-acceptance. The man only has one camera, and potentially an unlimited number of people could contact the man intending to purchase. The court would therefore presume a lack of contractual intent. This is further supported by the wording used, such as 'may sell', and 'contact me if you *wish* to buy', which are not conducive with a contractual intent. Option A is incorrect as the advertisement is not an offer for sale, so it is not capable of being accepted. Option B is incorrect. Whilst it is correct that a postal acceptance is effective when posted, this is not applicable here, as there is no offer for the woman to accept. As the advertisement is an invitation to treat, there is no offer to revoke (therefore option D is incorrect). Option E is incorrect as the woman's response may constitute a request for information, rather than a counter-offer, so this is incorrect on that point. Further, as the advertisement is an invitation to treat, the woman's letter is likely to constitute an offer, which has been rejected by the man.

Did you choose the correct answer?   YES ☐   NO ☐

See *Revise SQE: Contract Law*, **Chapter 1** for a discussion of this area of law.

A16 of 90 (page 9)   Area of law assessed: Ethics and professional conduct

The correct answer was E. This is because the SRA Code of Conduct requires solicitors to notify the SRA promptly if they are subject to any criminal charge, conviction or caution to which the rules apply. Driving with excess alcohol is a criminal conviction that must be disclosed. Option A is incorrect as the time frame stated in the Code of Conduct is 'promptly'. Option B is incorrect as the conviction must be disclosed, because the solicitor must uphold public trust and confidence in the profession. Option C is incorrect as all relevant convictions must be reported; notification is not restricted to offences of dishonesty. Option D is incorrect as reporting is not discretionary; a solicitor must notify the SRA of any conviction.

Did you choose the correct answer?   YES ☐   NO ☐

See *Revise SQE: Ethics and Professional Conduct*, **Chapter 2** for a discussion of this area of law.

A17 of 90 (page 9)   Area of law assessed: Contract law

The correct answer was A. This is because damages for breach of contract are usually awarded on the expectation measure. This reflects the loss of bargain and seeks to put the innocent party into the position they would have been in had the contract not been breached. However, in this question, the loss of expectation is too speculative. Neither party will know or be able to prove how successful, and ultimately how profitable, the film would have been in had it been completed and released. As such, the court will likely award damages on the reliance measure and will seek to put the production company into the position they would have been in had they not entered into the contract. This will allow the recovery of their expenditure incurred both before and after the breach. Option B is incorrect as the expectation loss is too speculative on the facts. Option C is incorrect as, in such claims, the innocent party is able to recover wasted expenditure incurred *both before* and *after* the breach. The damages are not only limited to the expenditure incurred after the breach. Option D is incorrect as it would not be appropriate to award damages on this measure, given the speculative nature of the loss. Option E is incorrect as it is unlikely that the production company can quantify this loss. This is essentially claiming damages on the expectation measure, which is incorrect as explained in the answer to option A, above.

Did you choose the correct answer?   YES ☐   NO ☐

See *Revise SQE: Contract Law*, **Chapter 10** for a discussion of this area of law.

A18 of 90 (page 10)   **Area of law assessed: Tort law**

The correct answer was D. This is because the court uses almost a mathematical formula in considering lost chance claims. The court decides using the balance of probabilities. The claimant has an 88% chance of death and only a 12% chance of survival, therefore on the balance of probabilities the court will find that the claimant was unlikely to survive had the ambulance arrived on time in any event. Option A is incorrect as the police have not acted negligently. Option B is incorrect as the court would not take underfunding into consideration – only the principles of negligence. Option C is incorrect as, although the court will accept the medical evidence, the claimant only had a 12% chance of survival. Option E is incorrect as contributory negligence is relevant only once primary liability has been found (in this case against the NHS) and the claimant has contributed to their injuries, which is not relevant here.

Did you choose the correct answer?   YES ☐   NO ☐

See *Revise SQE: Tort Law*, **Chapter 2** for a discussion of this area of law.

A19 of 90 (page 10)   **Area of law assessed: Contract law**

The correct answer was D. This is because the court has a discretion to allow a party to recover the value of any benefit conferred by the partial performance of a contract. Whilst this is at the court's discretion, as the company still have buyers for the tee-shirts, the court may award a just sum of £1,000 (representing the value of the tee-shirts delivered). At the time of frustration, the company had received half of the tee-shirts. There is no total failure of consideration, so a claim in restitution to reverse an unjust enrichment is not appropriate (therefore option A is incorrect). The effect of frustration is to discharge future obligations under the contract. As the requirement of the company to pay does not arise until after the frustrating event, the obligation for them to pay will be discharged (therefore option B is incorrect). The effect of frustration is to discharge the parties of their future obligations under the contract. The manufacturer will not be required to perform the contract after the contract is frustrated (therefore option C is incorrect). Option E is incorrect as there was no money paid or payable before the frustrating event, so an off-set of expenses is not appropriate in this scenario.

Did you choose the correct answer?   YES ☐   NO ☐

See *Revise SQE: Contract Law*, **Chapter 9** for a discussion of this area of law.

A20 of 90 (page 11)   **Area of law assessed: Dispute resolution**

The correct answer was C. This is because parties can appeal against an arbitrator's decision in limited circumstances (option E is therefore incorrect). The only basis upon which parties could appeal against the arbitrator's decision is if they felt that the law had been wrongly applied, and they need to seek permission of the court to make the appeal (therefore option B is incorrect). The arbitrator is under no obligation to reconsider any decision (option A is therefore incorrect) and neither party can request another arbitrator to reconsider the decision (therefore option D is incorrect).

Did you choose the correct answer?   YES ☐   NO ☐

See *Revise SQE: Dispute Resolution*, **Chapter 1** for a discussion of this area of law.

A21 of 90 (page 11)   **Area of law assessed: Legal services**

The correct answer was D. This is because the test for establishing whether professional indemnity insurance is adequate and appropriate is determined by a range of factors, including the size of the firm, the nature of the work undertaken by the firm and the possible value of any claims liabilities the firm may be exposed to. Because the firm is mid-sized and undertakes high-value serious injury claims, it may be exposed to substantial claims. A firm of this nature is unlikely to be able to meet the costs associated with such claims. As such, the level of professional indemnity insurance cover is unlikely to be deemed sufficient. All other options are therefore incorrect.

Did you choose the correct answer?   YES ☐   NO ☐

See *Revise SQE: The Legal System and Services of England and Wales*, **Chapter 5** for a discussion of this area of law.

A22 of 90 (page 12)   **Area of law assessed: Legal system of England and Wales and sources of law**

The correct answer was E. This is because judges may only refer to external aids to interpretation where the meaning of a statutory provision is ambiguous or lacks clarity. Options A and B are not the best available options because they do not make this clear. A judge may *only* refer to Hansard in cases where material from Hansard contains clear statements that were made by a minister regarding the meaning or scope of the relevant statute. The fact that the issue has been discussed recently in the House of Commons is therefore irrelevant, as is the fact that the Government has pledged to reform the law. Options B, C and D are therefore incorrect.

Did you choose the correct answer?   YES ☐   NO ☐

See *Revise SQE: The Legal System and Services of England and Wales*, **Chapter 3** for a discussion of this area of law.

A23 of 90 (page 12)   **Area of law assessed: Contract law**

The correct answer was B. This is because the courts apply an objective test to determine if a statement was intended to be binding and therefore whether it is a term of the contract. In this scenario there is a significant lapse of time and neither statement was reduced to writing. This would suggest lack of contractual intent, consistent with the statements being representations. The lapse of time and the fact neither statement is reduced to writing would create a strong presumption that the statements are representations (therefore option A is incorrect). Innominate terms are part of the agreement, and the seriousness of the breach will be used to determine whether the breach is treated as a breach of condition or warranty. On the facts of this scenario, the statements are likely to be representations and not legally binding (therefore option C is incorrect). Option D is incorrect as the lack of reliance by the man is not relevant to the determination. The parties may label statements as either conditions or warranties, but this is not conclusive (and therefore option E is incorrect). The court applies an objective test of intention to determine whether a statement is part of the contract and legally binding (therefore option A is incorrect).

Did you choose the correct answer?   YES ☐   NO ☐

See *Revise SQE: Contract Law*, **Chapter 5** for a discussion of this area of law.

A24 of 90 (page 13)   **Area of law assessed: Business law and practice**

The correct answer was A. This is because a fixed charge over stock is not appropriate as it is impractical for a business to seek permission from a lender to deal with the stock (which the terms of a fixed charge would require) – therefore options B and D would not be appropriate. A floating charge over machinery and stock would not be the most appropriate (for the lender at least, as it ranks lower in the statutory order of distribution on insolvency) – therefore option C is not appropriate. Option E is not part of a usual security offering in this situation, and is therefore incorrect.

Did you choose the correct answer?   YES ☐   NO ☐

See *Revise SQE: Business Law and Practice*, **Chapter 5** for a discussion of this area of law.

A25 of 90 (page 13)   **Area of law assessed: Business law and practice**

The correct answer was A. This is because option A is an incorrect statement purely on the figures – 17.5% × 2 = 35% which is more than a third. Options B, D and E all state that these things 'can' be achieved (often by inclusion in partnership agreement). Option C is a correct statement of advice in order to allow the friend to earn interest on capital, but this must be included in an agreement as the Partnership Act 1890 does not provide for it.

Did you choose the correct answer?   YES ☐   NO ☐

See *Revise SQE: Business Law and Practice*, **Chapter 2** for a discussion of this area of law.

A26 of 90 (page 14)   **Area of law assessed: Dispute resolution**

The correct answer was E. This is because the governing law is English law as the collision occurred in that jurisdiction. This makes options A, B and C incorrect. As the proposed defendant is habitually resident in Belgium and the damages flowing from the negligent act occurred in England and Wales, the client has the option to choose which jurisdiction in which to issue proceedings (therefore option D is incorrect).

Did you choose the correct answer?   YES ☐   NO ☐

See *Revise SQE: Dispute Resolution*, **Chapter 3** for a discussion of this area of law.

A27 of 90 (page 14)   **Area of law assessed: Constitutional and administrative law and EU law**

The correct answer was D. This is because the UK Parliament is the sovereign law-making body in respect of all non-devolved matters. Youth justice is not a devolved matter. This means that laws concerning youth justice policy would automatically come into effect in Welsh law. Option A is incorrect because it does not make clear that the Welsh Parliament has the power to make law in respect of devolved matters. Options B and C are incorrect because the consent or approval of the Welsh Parliament is not required to bring UK law into effect in Welsh law. Similarly, Option E is incorrect because UK law will come into effect in Welsh law providing it has been enacted through the usual legislative process.

Did you choose the correct answer?   YES ☐   NO ☐

See *Revise SQE: Constitutional and Administrative Law*, **Chapter 1** for a discussion of this area of law.

A28 of 90 (page 15)   **Area of law assessed: Tort law**

The correct answer was B. This is because under the Fatal Accidents Act 1976 (an authority that you do not need to know for the purposes of the SQE), a civil partner and any children treated by the deceased as a child of the family can bring a claim for dependency as long as the deceased provided for them financially. Options A, C and D are therefore incorrect. Option E is incorrect as, irrespective of the anaesthetist's experience, they will be judged to the standard of a professional anaesthetist and failure to monitor the claimant's oxygen is negligent.

Did you choose the correct answer?   YES ☐   NO ☐

See *Revise SQE: Tort Law*, **Chapter 3** for a discussion of this area of law.

A29 of 90 (page 15)   **Area of law assessed: Business law and practice**

The correct answer was C. This is because a company will pay corporation tax on its trading profits and capital gains. Only option C falls into this category; the other options fall outside this and are not subject to corporation tax.

Did you choose the correct answer?   YES ☐   NO ☐

See *Revise SQE: Business Law and Practice*, **Chapter 10** for a discussion of this area of law.

A30 of 90 (page 15)   **Area of law assessed: Contract law**

The correct answer was B. This is because the owner did not represent or warrant the painting to the work of a famous artist. The woman made a mistake as to the value of the painting, but this mistake will not render the contract void. In order to be void for mistake as to quality, the woman needs to establish that the lack of quality rendered the contract essentially different from what she believed it to be. She paid for and received the painting on the wall. In the absence of any representation or warranty, the woman will have no remedy in the law of mistake. This is a case of *caveat emptor* (buyer beware). Option A is incorrect as the painting was not described as being the work of a famous artist. Both the buyer and seller made a common mistake as to that fact, but this will not render the contract void. Option C is incorrect as a mistake on price alone will not render the contract void. Rescission of the contract is a possible remedy for misrepresentation. However, as noted above, the owner gave no representation or warranty that the painting was the work of a famous artist (option D is therefore incorrect). The price was agreed between the parties in the mistaken belief that it was by a famous artist. However, there was no representation or warranty to that fact. A mistake as to the price of the painting will not render the contract void or voidable. The contract for the sale of the painting was not essentially different than both parties believed it to be, and there was no misrepresentation as to the subject matter of the contract (therefore option E is incorrect).

Did you choose the correct answer?   YES ☐   NO ☐

See *Revise SQE: Contract Law*, **Chapter 8** for a discussion of this area of law.

A31 of 90 (page 16)   **Area of law assessed: Business law and practice**

The correct answer was D. This is because options C and E are forms to be filed when information is updated with Companies House after incorporation. Option A is not a requirement as, if no articles of association are filed, the model articles will be adopted as default. Option B is included in option D now, but on its own is not sufficient (therefore cannot be the best answer).

Did you choose the correct answer?   YES ☐   NO ☐

See *Revise SQE: Business Law and Practice*, **Chapter 3** for a discussion of this area of law.

A32 of 90 (page 16)   Area of law assessed: Business law and practice

The correct answer was B. This is because, in order to be a preference, the recipient must be placed in a better position as a result of the payment, there must be a desire to prefer this creditor over others on the part of the payer (unless the recipient is a connected person) and the payment must have been made within six months of the date of insolvency (two years for a connected person). Here, there is no desire to prefer because, instead, the payment has been made under a real threat of insolvency proceedings (statutory demand). The requirement for these criteria to be satisfied therefore rules out option C as a possible answer. There is no suggestion of fraud here so option D does not describe the likely position of the administrator. Options A and E are not viable options open to an administrator: option A is not viable because there needs to be more information about the company's situation (other than it was insolvent); option E because the payment will not be protected simply because it was made in the normal course of business and in good faith, eg, it could still amount to a preferential payment.

Did you choose the correct answer?   YES ☐   NO ☐

See *Revise SQE: Business Law and Practice*, **Chapter 6** for a discussion of this area of law.

A33 of 90 (page 17)   Area of law assessed: Business law and practice

The correct answer was A. This is because limited liability for debts is an advantage because the business will incur debt as it buys materials and will not be able to pay those bills if its own customers do not pay – that debt remains the business's rather than the shareholders'. In a partnership, the liability of the partners is unlimited. Therefore, option C does not represent the best advice. As the client wants to attract finance, a company or limited liability partnership (LLP) would be better than a partnership because they can grant floating charges. A company has a perceived higher status than an LLP and is more widely recognised worldwide, which would benefit the client in attracting international business. As options B, D and E reference starting an LLP, these do not represent the best advice to the client.

Did you choose the correct answer?   YES ☐   NO ☐

See *Revise SQE: Business Law and Practice*, **Chapter 1** for a discussion of this area of law.

A34 of 90 (page 17)   Area of law assessed: Legal services

The correct answer was A. This is because solicitors are under a duty to report any concerns about money laundering to the firm's nominated officer. The nominated officer will report any suspicious activity to the National Crime Agency. Options B and C are incorrect because they state that the solicitor should continue with the transaction. If the solicitor continued with the transaction, they are likely to commit an offence under anti-money laundering legislation. Options D and E are incorrect because they state that the solicitor should inform the client of their concerns. The solicitor should not do this because it could constitute an offence under anti-money laundering legislation.

Did you choose the correct answer?   YES ☐   NO ☐

See *Revise SQE: The Legal System and Services of England and Wales*, **Chapter 6** for a discussion of this area of law.

A35 of 90 (page 18)   **Area of law assessed: Business law and practice**

The correct answer was E. This is because a lender to any business will make its decision to lend based on the creditworthiness of the borrower that should be able to demonstrate solvency, ability to repay any loan and may be required to provide security. The only feasible option here is E. Options A, B and C are wholly unsuitable for this business (the client wishes to work alone and it is a start-up). As a sole trader, the client cannot grant a floating charge (therefore, option D is incorrect).

Did you choose the correct answer?   YES ☐   NO ☐

See *Revise SQE: Business Law and Practice*, **Chapter 5** for a discussion of this area of law.

A36 of 90 (page 18)   **Area of law assessed: Dispute resolution**

The correct answer was E. This is because this MCQ features a latent damage claim in tort, the limitation period for which is either six years from when the damage occurred, or three years from when the claimant (the client in this MCQ) first knew about the cause of action. This means that options A, B and C are incorrect. With latent damages claims, an action needs to be brought within 15 years of the date on which the negligent act took place, therefore making option D incorrect.

Did you choose the correct answer?   YES ☐   NO ☐

See *Revise SQE: Dispute Resolution*, **Chapter 2** for a discussion of this area of law.

A37 of 90 (page 19)   **Area of law assessed: Constitutional and administrative law and EU law**

The correct answer was D. This is because the King's powers to dismiss the Prime Minister are restricted by convention. The King, under the Royal Prerogative, has the power to appoint the Prime Minister. The King could therefore dismiss the Prime Minister from office if he wished to do so. However, by convention the Prime Minister will remain in office if they maintain the support of the majority of the House of Commons. In this scenario, the Prime Minister still enjoys the support of the majority of the House of Commons so the convention would apply (option B is therefore incorrect). Options A and C are incorrect because they do not make any reference to the applicable convention. Option E is incorrect because the King does have the power to appoint the Prime Minister under the Royal Prerogative.

Did you choose the correct answer?   YES ☐   NO ☐

See *Revise SQE: Constitutional and Administrative Law*, **Chapter 4** for a discussion of this area of law.

A38 of 90 (page 19)   **Area of law assessed: Business law and practice**

The correct answer was C. This is because each partner is jointly and severally liable for all the debts of the partnership if a partnership becomes insolvent. This means that they stand to lose not only what they have invested in the business (therefore option A is incorrect) but also any other property they own, as creditors of the partnership can pursue any one of the individual partners until the debts are paid. The client's liability is potentially unlimited. The partnership agreement may make provision as to how losses are to be shared but this does not prevent a creditor claiming in full from one partner who would then have to claim against the others (therefore options B, D and E are incorrect).

Did you choose the correct answer?   YES ☐   NO ☐

See *Revise SQE: Business Law and Practice*, **Chapter 6** for a discussion of this area of law.

A39 of 90 (page 20)   Area of law assessed: **Dispute resolution**

The correct answer was A. This is because for personal injury claims which have complex facts and are worth over £50,000, the High Court is the correct court to issue proceedings. £100,000 is the County Court limit for all claims except personal injury, meaning options B, D and E are incorrect. Option C is incorrect because we are told that the facts surrounding both liability and quantum are complex.

Did you choose the correct answer?   YES ☐   NO ☐

See *Revise SQE: Dispute Resolution*, **Chapter 3** for a discussion of this area of law.

A40 of 90 (page 20)   Area of law assessed: **Legal services**

The correct answer was B. This is because the solicitor is under a duty to report any concerns to the firm's nominated officer. The solicitor disclosed her concerns to the nominated officer, and this is likely to be enough to discharge her legal obligations under anti-money laundering legislation (options A and D are therefore incorrect). The solicitor is not under a duty to make a Suspicious Activity Report (SAR) to the National Crime Agency (NCA) so she has not committed an offence under anti-money laundering legislation (option C is therefore incorrect). The duty to make a SAR to the NCA rests with the firm's nominated officer. Option E is incorrect because the report the solicitor made to the firm's nominated officer is not a SAR.

Did you choose the correct answer?   YES ☐   NO ☐

See *Revise SQE: The Legal System and Services of England and Wales*, **Chapter 6** for a discussion of this area of law.

A41 of 90 (page 21)   Area of law assessed: **Legal system of England and Wales and sources of law**

The correct answer was A. This is because the law was in force on 31 January 2020. This date is known as the 'exit date' because it is when the UK ceased to be a member of the EU. All EU law in effect on exit day is classified as retained EU law. It is important to remember that the definition of EU retained law is any EU law that was in effect on exit day and not EU law which was in effect on completion date (31 December 2020). Option E is therefore incorrect. Options B, C and D are all incorrect because they misstate the concept of EU retained law.

Did you choose the correct answer?   YES ☐   NO ☐

See *Revise SQE: Constitutional and Administrative Law*, **Chapter 9** for a discussion of this area of law.

A42 of 90 (page 22)   Area of law assessed: **Contract law**

The correct answer was D. This is because the court will presume that the dealership only intended to deal with the party named in the document as the man signs the sales agreement in the name of Mr Smith. As the man was not the party named in the document, Mr Smith, the contract will be void for mistake (option A is therefore incorrect). A contract that is voidable still binds the parties until steps are taken to set it aside. In a claim for misrepresentation, it is therefore unlikely that the dealership could recover the car from the woman. Property will have passed from the dealership to the man, and then from the man to the woman. Once a third party acquires rights under a contract this is likely to bar a claim for rescission of the contract (therefore, option B is incorrect). As the contract is void for mistake, no property would have passed along the chain from the dealership to the woman (option C is therefore incorrect). It is correct that the woman has also been the victim of fraud. Her remedy, therefore, will be against the man. As it is unlikely that the woman will be able to identify or locate the man, she will have no effective remedy (option E is therefore incorrect).

Did you choose the correct answer?   YES ☐   NO ☐

See *Revise SQE: Contract Law*, **Chapter 8** for a discussion of this area of law.

A43 of 90 (page 22)   Area of law assessed: Legal services

The correct answer was C. This is because the SRA Code of Conduct requires the solicitor to report all potential breaches of confidentiality to the firm's Compliance Officer for Legal Practice (COLP). Although the solicitor has reported the potential breach to a senior member of staff, she is required to report the potential breach to the COLP (options A and E are therefore incorrect). Failure to make a report to the COLP will amount to a breach of the Code of Conduct. The fact that she is not yet a fully qualified solicitor does not impact her liability under the Code of Conduct (option D is therefore incorrect). Option B is not the best available answer because it does not clearly outline that the solicitor is under a duty to report the potential breach to the COLP.

Did you choose the correct answer?   YES ☐   NO ☐

See *Revise SQE: The Legal System and Services of England and Wales*, **Chapter 5** for a discussion of this area of law.

A44 of 90 (page 22)   Area of law assessed: Ethics and professional conduct

The correct answer was C. This is because the SRA Code of Conduct requires solicitors to report promptly to the SRA any facts or matters that they reasonably believe are capable of amounting to a serious breach of their regulatory arrangements by any person regulated by them. Harassment would meet this definition. The *best* approach that can be taken is for the solicitor to inform the Compliance Officer for Legal Practice (COLP) *and* inform the Solicitors Regulation Authority (SRA) as to the alleged harassment. Options A and B are incorrect as the *best* advice is to notify both the COLP and the SRA. Option D is not appropriate in light of the above obligation under the Code and option E would not be the most sensible decision, given the likely risk of victimisation and further harassment.

Did you choose the correct answer?   YES ☐   NO ☐

See *Revise SQE: Ethics and Professional Conduct*, **Chapter 2** for a discussion of this area of law.

A45 of 90 (page 23)   Area of law assessed: Contract law

The correct answer was E. This is because an award of £2,000 represents the normal loss that would have been in the reasonable contemplation of the supplier when entering the contract. The lucrative contract with the vineyard is likely to be classified as abnormal loss. This loss was not communicated to the suppliers. It is unlikely to be within their reasonable contemplation and therefore too remote. An award of £20,000 represents the amount agreed in the contract. These are referred to as liquidated damages. In order for a liquidated damages clause to be binding, it needs to represent a genuine pre-estimate of loss. On the facts, £20,000 seems to be an extravagant amount compared to the maximum loss suffered. It is unlikely to be enforceable and the court will award the company unliquidated damages (therefore option A is incorrect). An award of £12,000 represents both the normal and abnormal loss suffered by the company. It is likely that the abnormal loss will be too remote, and unrecoverable, as noted above (option B is therefore incorrect). An award of £10,000 represents an award for the abnormal loss only. It is likely that only the normal loss would have been in the supplier's reasonable contemplation (option C is therefore incorrect). An award of £8,000 represents the difference between the normal and abnormal loss. This is not in accordance with the usual measure of damages in contract, which seeks to protect the expectation interest (option D is therefore incorrect).

Did you choose the correct answer?   YES ☐   NO ☐

See *Revise SQE: Contract Law*, **Chapter 10** for a discussion of this area of law.

A46 of 90 (page 23)   Area of law assessed: Tort law

The correct answer was B. This is because damage to the property of a third party (namely the motorway barriers) has caused economic loss to the woman and is not recoverable. Option A is incorrect as the loss of the woman's job prospects is not consequential loss. Option C is incorrect as no duty of care is owed and the woman cannot claim for economic loss. Option D is incorrect as the woman has not suffered consequential loss but economic loss. Option E is incorrect as the lorry driver did not owe a duty of care to the woman as there is no relationship between the parties.

Did you choose the correct answer?   YES ☐   NO ☐

See *Revise SQE: Tort Law*, **Chapter 3** for a discussion of this area of law.

A47 of 90 (page 24)   Area of law assessed: Dispute resolution

The correct answer was D. This is because the document in question is a claim form, which is deemed served two business days after the relevant step is taken (therefore option A is incorrect). In this case, the relevant step is posting the claim form through the defendant's letterbox. As the relevant step is taken on a Friday, this is counted as a business day, meaning that the second business day is Monday (therefore option E is incorrect). Saturday and Sunday are not business days (therefore options B and C are incorrect).

Did you choose the correct answer?   YES ☐   NO ☐

See *Revise SQE: Dispute Resolution*, **Chapter 3** for a discussion of this area of law.

A48 of 90 (page 24)   Area of law assessed: Contract law

The correct answer was A. This is because the woman is acting as a consumer and the car dealer is acting as a trader. The contract is a 'consumer' contract and will include an implied term that the goods are of satisfactory quality. This is a condition of the contract. A breach of condition entitles the woman to reject the goods and to claim a full refund. She does not have to accept the offer of repair. Option B is incorrect as the serious defect within the engine will be seen as a breach of a condition of the contract. The woman has the right to reject the goods. Option C is incorrect as the breach of contract is caused by the defect in the engine. The goods were not of satisfactory quality. Option D is incorrect as the goods are expected to last for a reasonable period of time without defect. The fact that the fault was discovered so quickly is evidence that the goods were not of satisfactory quality. Option E is incorrect as the reason that the car will not start is due to the defect in the engine. The goods were not of satisfactory quality.

Did you choose the correct answer?   YES ☐   NO ☐

See *Revise SQE: Contract Law*, **Chapter 5** for a discussion of this area of law.

A49 of 90 (page 25)   Area of law assessed: Legal services

The correct answer was A. This is because a legal executive may carry on reserved legal activities under the instruction and supervision of a solicitor who is authorised to carry on such activities. Option C is incorrect because legal executives may only carry on some reserved legal activities. Option B is incorrect because legal executives are classified as legal service providers. Legal executives do not need to have practice rights to carry on reserved legal activities if they are carrying on such activities under the instruction and supervision of a solicitor who is authorised to carry on such activities (option E is therefore incorrect). Option D is incorrect because legal executives are regulated by Chartered Institute of Legal Executives (CILEx) and not the SRA.

Did you choose the correct answer?   YES ☐   NO ☐

See *Revise SQE: The Legal System and Services of England and Wales*, **Chapter 5** for a discussion of this area of law.

A50 of 90 (page 25)   Area of law assessed: Legal system of England and Wales and sources of law

The correct answer was A. This is because solicitors are granted rights of audience automatically when they are admitted to the roll of solicitors. Solicitors may not exercise rights of audience in senior courts unless the solicitor has completed the relevant education and training required by the Solicitors Regulation Authority and been awarded higher rights of audience. The magistrates' court is *not* a senior court. This means that the solicitor does not need to have been awarded higher rights of audience to appear on behalf of their client in the magistrates' court (options B, D and E are therefore incorrect). Option C is incorrect because a solicitor's right to exercise rights of audience is not determined by judicial consent.

Did you choose the correct answer?   YES ☐   NO ☐

See *Revise SQE: The Legal System and Services of England and Wales*, **Chapter 1** for a discussion of this area of law.

A51 of 90 (page 26)   Area of law assessed: Contract law

The correct answer was C. This is because the courts are generally hostile to a clause that seeks to exclude liability. As such, they will favour an interpretation that goes against the party wishing to rely on the clause. This is known as the *contra proferentem* rule. Option A is incorrect as the courts will prefer an interpretation that goes *against* the party wishing to rely on the clause, and not in their favour. In seeking to prevent any abuse of bargaining position, the courts adopt a strict interpretation against the party relying on the clause and will not rewrite the agreement based on what a reasonable person would have intended (option B is therefore incorrect). Option D is incorrect as, whilst this approach may be used generally to determine the issue of contractual intent, the court generally adopts the *contra proferentem* rule in relation to exclusion clauses.

Option E is incorrect as this approach is more representative of a general approach to statutory interpretation and to the specific use of exclusion clauses.

Did you choose the correct answer?   YES ☐   NO ☐

See *Revise SQE: Contract Law*, **Chapter 6** for a discussion of this area of law.

A52 of 90 (page 26)   Area of law assessed: Ethics and professional conduct

The correct answer was A. This is because the SRA Code of Conduct imposes an obligation on solicitors to: report promptly, to the SRA, any facts or matters that they reasonably believe are capable of amounting to a serious breach of their regulatory arrangements by any person regulated by them (including themselves). Option B is incorrect because such a breach would not be reported directly to the client; furthermore, the requirement to report is based on 'serious breach' and not 'misconduct or other reprehensible behaviour' (for this reason, option E is incorrect). Option C is incorrect as the serious breach need not be a criminal offence. Option D is incorrect because the report must be made to the SRA, not the client.

Did you choose the correct answer?   YES ☐   NO ☐

See *Revise SQE: Ethics and Professional Conduct*, **Chapter 2** for a discussion of this area of law

A53 of 90 (page 27)   Area of law assessed: Tort law

The correct answer was E. This is because the court uses the egg-shell skull theory (take your victim as you find them); this means that the defendant must accept injuries caused to the claimant despite the pre-existing medical issue. Option A is incorrect as the court will only reduce damages if they find the claimant contributed to their injuries and this is not the case here. Option B is incorrect as the employer was liable due to lack of training. Option C is incorrect because the previous back injury predates the accident at work and therefore is unable to break the chain of causation. Option D is incorrect as the court has to take the claimant as they find them, namely with a vulnerable back.

Did you choose the correct answer?   YES ☐   NO ☐

See *Revise SQE: Tort Law*, **Chapter 3** for a discussion of this area of law.

A54 of 90 (page 27)   Area of law assessed: Legal services

The correct answer was E. This is because in circumstances where a firm fails to renew its policy by the expiry date it will automatically enter an extended policy period (EPP). The EPP lasts for 30 days from the policy expiry date. During this period the firm may continue to act on behalf of its clients. Option D is incorrect because it states that the firm may act for its clients for the next 30 days. This is incorrect because the EPP starts from the date the policy expired. Options A, B and C are incorrect because they do not take into account the fact that the EPP came into effect when the policy elapsed. Option C ignores the fact that the firm has five working days to notify the SRA that it has entered an EPP.

Did you choose the correct answer?   YES ☐   NO ☐

See *Revise SQE: The Legal System and Services of England and Wales*, **Chapter 5** for a discussion of this area of law.

A55 of 90 (page 28)   **Area of law assessed: Dispute resolution**

The correct answer was A. This is because the claimant is able to make an application for default judgment here (therefore options D and E are incorrect). The defendant has 14 days to acknowledge service or file a defence, after which the claimant is free to submit an application for default judgment (therefore option B is incorrect). An application is made by completing the relevant form (N244) and sending this to the court with the appropriate fee (making option C incorrect).

Did you choose the correct answer?   YES ☐   NO ☐

See *Revise SQE: Dispute Resolution*, **Chapter 4** for a discussion of this area of law.

A56 of 90 (page 28)   **Area of law assessed: Legal services**

The correct answer was C. This is because the limit on disposable income to qualify for civil legal aid is £733 or less. As the woman has a disposable income of £800, she does not satisfy the means test. The woman's gross income is £2,500 which is less than the limit (£2,657), and her disposable capital is £6,000 which is below the limit of £8,000. As a result, all other options are incorrect.

Did you choose the correct answer?   YES ☐   NO ☐

See *Revise SQE: The Legal System and Services of England and Wales*, **Chapter 8** for a discussion of this area of law.

A57 of 90 (page 29)   **Area of law assessed: Dispute resolution**

The correct answer was E. This is because the mandatory ground is not applicable here (therefore, option B is incorrect) and the application should be made promptly (making options C and D incorrect). The applicant is only required to show either that they have a reasonable prospect of successfully defending the claim or there is a good reason why they did not respond (therefore, option A is incorrect).

Did you choose the correct answer?   YES ☐   NO ☐

See *Revise SQE: Dispute Resolution*, **Chapter 4** for a discussion of this area of law.

A58 of 90 (page 29)   **Area of law assessed: Tort law**

The correct answer was E. This is because the claimant has suffered a medically diagnosed psychiatric condition and would be classed as a primary victim as they were directly outside the property that exploded and, although not physically injured, could have been. Option A is incorrect as the claimant is a primary victim. Option C is incorrect as the claimant did not suffer physical injury. Option B is incorrect as the claimant is in the zone of physical danger as they are directly outside the property that exploded and we are aware that several houses were destroyed. Option D is incorrect as a tie of love and affection relates to secondary victims and the claimant is a primary victim.

Did you choose the correct answer?   YES ☐   NO ☐

See *Revise SQE: Tort Law*, **Chapter 3** for a discussion of this area of law.

A59 of 90 (page 30)   **Area of law assessed: Legal system of England and Wales and sources of law**

The correct answer was D. This is because the Supreme Court may consider appeals from the High Court where the leapfrog procedure is applicable (option C is therefore incorrect). The leapfrog procedure can only be used where the decision concerns a point of law of general public importance *and* the decision is unlikely to be of particular significance, raises issues of national importance or the benefits of early consideration by the Supreme Court outweigh the benefits of consideration by the Court of Appeal (option B is therefore incorrect). Option A is incorrect because the value of the claim is irrelevant to the leapfrog criteria. Because the scenario clearly states that the outcome of the case is unlikely to be of particular significance and does not raise issues of national importance, the procedure would only be available if the benefits of early consideration by the Supreme Court outweigh the benefits of consideration by the Court of Appeal. Option E is incorrect because it misstates the leapfrog criteria. On the facts provided, there is no reason to believe that the benefits of early consideration outweigh the benefits of the case being considered by the Court of Appeal, so Option D is the best available answer.

Did you choose the correct answer?   YES ☐   NO ☐

See *Revise SQE: The Legal System and Services of England and Wales*, **Chapter 1** for a discussion of this area of law.

A60 of 90 (page 30)   **Area of law assessed: Constitutional and administrative law and EU law**

The correct answer was A. This is because the disclosure would be protected under parliamentary privilege. Parliamentary privilege grants certain legal immunities to members of both Houses of Parliament and this includes protection from any civil action that would ordinarily arise as a result of such disclosures/statements. Statements and disclosures made during the course of ordinary parliamentary proceedings are covered by parliamentary privilege. Options C, D and E are incorrect because they all state that the disclosure would fall outside the scope of parliamentary privilege. Option B is incorrect because it does not address parliamentary privilege and implies that the member of the House of Lords would be liable for breaching the injunction.

Did you choose the correct answer?   YES ☐   NO ☐

See *Revise SQE: Constitutional and Administrative Law*, **Chapter 2** for a discussion of this area of law.

A61 of 90 (page 31)   **Area of law assessed: Legal services**

The correct answer was D. This is because the business will not need to have Professional Indemnity Insurance (PII) if it is not engaged in any reserved legal activities. Will writing is not a reserved legal activity. Option A is incorrect because the duty to have cover of up to £3 million for any one claim only applies to firms carrying on reserved legal activities. Options B, C and E are incorrect because the requirement that PII is both adequate and appropriate does not apply to the business. Options B and C would have been incorrect in any event because they do not accurately set out the minimum PII threshold.

Did you choose the correct answer?   YES ☐   NO ☐

See *Revise SQE: The Legal System and Services of England and Wales*, **Chapter 5** for a discussion of this area of law.

A52 of 90 (page 31)   **Area of law assessed: Ethics and professional conduct**

The correct answer was B. This is because the SRA Code of Conduct prohibits a solicitor from acting in circumstances where there is a conflict of interest or a significant risk of such a conflict between current and new clients. The exception to this rule (where clients are competing for the same objective) does not apply because the current client has clearly stated that the solicitor cannot act for another party to these proceedings (which the solicitor has accepted through the retainer). Therefore, the current client would not consent to this course of conduct (option E is incorrect). Option A is incorrect because the solicitor must not act without disclosing the conflict of interest. Option C is incorrect because the solicitor owes a duty to act in the best interests of each client; to withdraw their services simply because another client is offering more money would not be acting in the current client's best interests. Option D is incorrect because this is not an own interest conflict case.

Did you choose the correct answer?   YES ☐   NO ☐

See *Revise SQE: Ethics and Professional Conduct*, **Chapter 2** for a discussion of this area of law.

A53 of 90 (page 32)   **Area of law assessed: Contract law**

The correct answer was C. This is because the employee has strictly not provided consideration to the insurer as the contract is between the employer and the insurer. However, as a matter of convenience, the money is channelled through the employer. This provides an exception for the need to provide direct consideration and creates a presumption that the employee has the right to enforce the contract. As this is a contract of convenience (the payment is given to the employer rather than each employee having to make payment directly to the insurer) there is no need for the employee to provide consideration directly to the insurer (option A is therefore incorrect). Option B is incorrect as there are exceptions to the privity of contract rule in contracts of convenience. Option D is incorrect as in a contract of convenience there is no need for the employee to provide consideration directly to the insurer. As the employee is presumed to have rights of enforceability, the employer cannot withhold the payment (option E is therefore incorrect).

Did you choose the correct answer?   YES ☐   NO ☐

See *Revise SQE: Contract Law*, **Chapter 4** for a discussion of this area of law.

A54 of 90 (page 32)   **Area of law assessed: Dispute resolution**

The correct answer was C. This is because an acknowledgement of service needs to be filed within 14 days of the date of service of the claim form and particulars of claim (therefore options A and B are incorrect). Provided this is done, this extends the period within which a defence (and in this case counterclaim) must be filed to 28 days from date of service of the claim form and particulars of claim (therefore, options D and E incorrect).

Did you choose the correct answer?   YES ☐   NO ☐

See *Revise SQE: Dispute Resolution*, **Chapter 4** for a discussion of this area of law.

A55 of 90 (page 33)   **Area of law assessed: Ethics and professional conduct**

The correct answer was E. This is because whilst all of the Principles may be relevant to this scenario, the Principle to act with independence is the most prominent. As a solicitor, it is essential to maintain independence and avoid conflicts of interest. In this scenario, the solicitor has a personal relationship with an employee of the competitor, which creates an own interest conflict. The solicitor must ensure that their independence is not compromised and that they provide unbiased legal advice and representation to the client. Therefore, whilst all five of these Principles may be relevant, and are of importance, the Principle to act with independence is likely to be the most relevant. All other options are therefore incorrect.

Did you choose the correct answer?   YES ☐   NO ☐

See *Revise SQE: Ethics and Professional Conduct*, **Chapter 1** for a discussion of this area of law.

A66 of 90 (page 33)   Area of law assessed: Business law and practice

The correct answer was D. This is because the client is a higher rate taxpayer (ie, the client's taxable income exceeds the basic rate threshold level set by HMRC). Therefore, options A and C are immediately excluded because these would only apply if the client had a taxable income that fell entirely within the basic rate band. Option E is incorrect in law – individuals do pay income tax on dividends received from a trading company. Option B is incorrect as it fails to take account of the dividend allowance – the statement implies that the client's entire dividend income would be taxed at the higher rate of income tax and ignores the ability of the client to pay 0% on the amount of dividend income within the dividend allowance.

Did you choose the correct answer?   YES ☐   NO ☐

See *Revise SQE: Business Law and Practice*, **Chapter 8** for a discussion of this area of law.

A67 of 90 (page 33)   Area of law assessed: Legal system of England and Wales and sources of law

The correct answer was B. This is because High Court judges have jurisdiction to sit in the High Court, the Crown Court and the Family Court. Options A, C, D and E are therefore incorrect.

Did you choose the correct answer?   YES ☐   NO ☐

See *Revise SQE: The Legal System and Services of England and Wales*, **Chapter 1** for a discussion of this area of law.

A68 of 90 (page 34)   Area of law assessed: Dispute resolution

The correct answer was A. This is because it is immaterial that the facts of the case are different from those in the original claim; the defendant is still entitled to bring a counterclaim against the claimant without needing to issue proceedings separately (options B, C and D are therefore incorrect). Option E is incorrect as the time period within which the defendant could file the counterclaim has not expired. It can therefore be filed at the same time as the defence without the court's permission.

Did you choose the correct answer?   YES ☐   NO ☐

See *Revise SQE: Dispute Resolution*, **Chapter 5** for a discussion of this area of law.

A69 of 90 (page 35)   Area of law assessed: Contract law

The correct answer was E. This is because the provision of the staff development will constitute sufficient consideration. The training was never part of the original agreement. The only obligation of the business was to repay the loan in accordance with the agreement. By providing the staff development, the business is going beyond their existing obligations. This is an exception to the common law rule that part-payment of a debt is generally insufficient as consideration. The principles developed by the Court of Appeal in *Williams v Roffey*, and the recognition that a practical benefit may constitute valuable consideration, are limited to contracts for goods and/or services. They cannot apply to the part-payment of a debt (therefore option A is incorrect). Option B is incorrect as the staff training may have economic value even though no payment was given in exchange. The doctrine of promissory estoppel is an equitable remedy that may provide a defence when a party has relied upon a promise. However, in this scenario, recourse to equity would not be appropriate. The staff training will constitute valuable consideration and the lender's promise is binding at common law (option C is therefore incorrect). Option D is incorrect as it represents the general position at common law. However, there are exceptions to this general rule. Evidence that a party has gone beyond what was required under the contract, such as the provision of a service in exchange for the promise to accept a lesser amount, will constitute good consideration.

Did you choose the correct answer?   YES ☐   NO ☐

See *Revise SQE: Contract Law*, **Chapter 2** for a discussion of this area of law.

A70 of 90 (page 35)   Area of law assessed: Legal services

The correct answer was D. This is because the conduct is a clear example of direct discrimination on the basis of sex and age. Options A, B and C are incorrect because they do not classify the conduct as direct discrimination. Option E is incorrect because positive discrimination refers to situations where an employer treats a person/people more favourably because of a protected characteristic. This is not applicable here because any female applicants aged 25 to 35 are not being treated favourably.

Did you choose the correct answer?   YES ☐   NO ☐

See *Revise SQE: The Legal System and Services of England and Wales*, **Chapter 6** for a discussion of this area of law.

A71 of 90 (page 36)   Area of law assessed: Tort law

The correct answer was A. This is because the court will find on balance that the defendant is no longer acting in the course of their employment, by using a firework and also due to the fact that they have left work. Option B is incorrect for the same reason, namely that the defendant has left work and is no longer acting in the course of their employment; option B is also incorrect as it is irrelevant that the defendant does not work for the manufacturing plant – the plant has subcontracted the defendant and thus has responsibility for them whilst on site. Option C is incorrect as there is not sufficient proximity and the defendant was not acting in the course of their employment. Option D is incorrect as throwing the firework causes the claimant to fall into the road; the chain of causation is not broken. Option E is incorrect as neither company are vicarious liable as the defendant was not acting in the course of their employment.

Did you choose the correct answer?   YES ☐   NO ☐

See *Revise SQE: Tort Law*, **Chapter 3** for a discussion of this area of law.

A72 of 90 (page 37)   **Area of law assessed: Contract law**

The correct answer was B. This is because the performance of an existing contractual duty will generally be insufficient as consideration. However, the Court of Appeal in *Williams v Roffey* recognised that performance of an existing contractual duty could constitute valuable consideration if that performance confers a practical benefit to the promisor. The company has gained no more in law than they were entitled to under the contract. Nevertheless, as a matter of fact, the company has avoided the operation of the penalty clause. This will be sufficient consideration under the principles developed in *Williams v Roffey*. Simple reliance upon a promise does not make it binding at common law (option A is therefore incorrect). As noted above, *Williams v Roffey* provides an exception to the general rule that performance of an existing contractual duty is insufficient consideration (therefore option C is incorrect). Option D is incorrect as there is no evidence on the facts that the builders have exceeded their contractual duty. The company are giving their promise of an additional payment in exchange for the builders completing the work on time. This is not an example of past consideration (option E is therefore incorrect).

Did you choose the correct answer?   YES ☐   NO ☐

See *Revise SQE: Contract Law*, **Chapter 2** for a discussion of this area of law.

A73 of 90 (page 37)   **Area of law assessed: Business law and practice**

The correct answer was B. This is because the transaction clearly falls within the definition of a substantial property transaction (SPT) from the Companies Act 2006. An STP is an arrangement under which a director (or connected person) acquires or is to acquire from the company a non-cash asset, or the company acquires or is to acquire from a director (or connected person) a non-cash asset where the value is substantial (ie, exceeds 10% of company's asset value and is more than £5,000 or it exceeds £100,000) and the consideration is cash. If the transaction fulfils this definition, the company needs to approve it by passing an ordinary resolution of the shareholders. If this approval is not obtained, the transaction is voidable. On this reasoning, option E is incorrect, and option C is incorrect as the transaction would be voidable (not void). Option D is incorrect in law as the declaration of interest would be required in addition to the other formalities described. Option A is incorrect as it includes reference to the inability to vote at a shareholders' meeting (he would be able to vote).

Did you choose the correct answer?   YES ☐   NO ☐

See *Revise SQE: Business Law and Practice*, **Chapter 4** for a discussion of this area of law.

A74 of 90 (page 38)   **Area of law assessed: Ethics and professional conduct**

The correct answer was B. This is because the SRA Code of Conduct requires solicitors to ensure that clients receive the best possible information about how their matter will be priced and about the likely overall cost of the matter and any costs incurred. This duty is a continuing one, arising at the time of engagement and as the matter progresses (therefore option E is incorrect). Given that the work of the colleague will incur extra costs, the solicitor must keep the client informed (therefore option A is incorrect). Option C is incorrect because the work of the colleague will amount to costs. Option D is incorrect because the SRA Code of Conduct does not dictate that the costs must be 'substantial', but that they must be kept informed 'when appropriate'. Additional costs by instructing the expert colleague is an appropriate circumstance.

Did you choose the correct answer?   YES ☐   NO ☐

See *Revise SQE: Ethics and Professional Conduct*, **Chapter 1** for a discussion of this area of law.

A75 of 90 (page 38)   **Area of law assessed: Constitutional and administrative law and EU law**

The correct answer was D. This is because notice must be given in advance of any procession. Typically, notice must be given at least six clear days before the procession is due to take place. Options A, B, C and E are incorrect because they do not correctly identify the usual notice period for processions.

Did you choose the correct answer?   YES ☐   NO ☐

See *Revise SQE: Constitutional and Administrative Law*, **Chapter 6** for a discussion of this area of law.

A76 of 90 (page 39)   **Area of law assessed: Business law and practice**

The correct answer was C. This is because options A, B, D and E all represent sources of income that can be excluded from the calculation. As option C would attract Capital Gains Tax, the profit cannot be so excluded.

Did you choose the correct answer?   YES ☐   NO ☐

See *Revise SQE: Business Law and Practice*, **Chapter 8** for a discussion of this area of law.

A77 of 90 (page 39)   **Area of law assessed: Ethics and professional conduct**

The correct answer was C. This is because the SRA Code of Conduct requires solicitors to act in the best interests of the client. The SRA Code of Conduct requires a solicitor to make the client aware of all information material to the matter of which they have knowledge. None of the exceptions to this rule apply, meaning that the client should be informed of the disadvantages of the dispute resolution clause (option A is therefore incorrect). The most appropriate action, therefore, is to inform the client of the potential drawbacks and seek instructions on how to proceed. Option B is incorrect as the solicitor must act in the best interests of the client, and the client must be informed of the drawbacks of the dispute resolution clause. Options D and E are incorrect as the information to the client must come *before* action is taken, and not *after*.

Did you choose the correct answer?   YES ☐   NO ☐

See *Revise SQE: Ethics and Professional Conduct*, **Chapter 1** for a discussion of this area of law.

A78 of 90 (page 40)   **Area of law assessed: Dispute resolution**

The correct answer was D. This is because the defendant should deal principally with the allegations that are made in the particulars of claim in his defence, but draw attention to inconsistencies between the two documents where appropriate (thus options C and E are incorrect). Although the burden of proof is on the claimant, the defendant should not just deny everything as this implies that he has knowledge of the facts (making options A and B incorrect).

Did you choose the correct answer?   YES ☐   NO ☐

See *Revise SQE: Dispute Resolution*, **Chapter 5** for a discussion of this area of law.

A79 of 90 (page 40)   Area of law assessed: **Business law and practice**

The correct answer was C. This is because in order to successfully apply to have a payment set aside on the grounds that it was a preference payment, it must be possible to establish or presume a desire to prefer. Option A is not a requirement. If option D is present, the payment is less likely to be set aside, particularly if it was made as a result of a threat of insolvency proceedings. Whilst options B and E may be present they are not essential, particularly if the payment was made to a connected person.

Did you choose the correct answer?   YES ☐   NO ☐

See *Revise SQE: Business Law and Practice*, **Chapter 6** for a discussion of this area of law.

A80 of 90 (page 41)   Area of law assessed: **Business law and practice**

The correct answer was B. This is because option A is too vague in that it does not fully explore the circumstances in which the partnership may be liable for the actions of the friend. Options C and D are incorrect statements as liability can arise in ways other than actual authority or all three partners agreeing. This is not an example of implied authority, therefore option E is incorrect.

Did you choose the correct answer?   YES ☐   NO ☐

See *Revise SQE: Business Law and Practice*, **Chapter 2** for a discussion of this area of law.

A81 of 90 (page 41)   Area of law assessed: **Dispute resolution**

The correct answer was D. This is because the test for a freezing injunction is whether there is a real risk of the defendant dissipating assets (therefore option E is incorrect), and it is appropriate to apply for a without notice hearing, given the risk of swift disposal if the defendant were to find out that a freezing injunction had been applied for (making options A and B incorrect). The evidence also suggests that the defendant is trying to transfer the asset to avoid payment of any judgment sum (therefore option C is incorrect).

Did you choose the correct answer?   YES ☐   NO ☐

See *Revise SQE: Dispute Resolution*, **Chapter 6** for a discussion of this area of law.

A82 of 90 (page 42)   Area of law assessed: **Tort law**

The correct answer was C. This is because the requirement for more haircuts is a choice and not a consequence of the accident or the defendant's negligence. Options A and B are incorrect because the court will not award an amount of damages for this head of loss. Option D is incorrect because the client did need to change their job due to the accident. Option E is incorrect because the increased frequency of haircuts is not as a direct effect of the defendant's negligence.

Did you choose the correct answer?   YES ☐   NO ☐

See *Revise SQE: Tort Law*, **Chapter 3** for a discussion of this area of law.

A83 of 90 (page 42)   Area of law assessed: **Legal system of England and Wales and sources of law**

The correct answer was C. This is because the Trade and Co-Operation Agreement (TCA) has legal effect in UK law: as part of the Withdrawal Agreement, Parliament permitted the EU to egislate for the UK for the limited purposes of the TCA. Because Parliament is the sovereign law-making body in the UK, it may withdraw this permission through an Act of Parliament if it wished to do so. Option A is incorrect because it expressly states that Parliament may not withdraw its permission under any circumstances. Option D is incorrect because it states that Parliament may choose to disapply the TCA, which is not possible under the terms of the Withdrawal Agreement. Similarly, Option B is incorrect because the Withdrawal Agreement does not give domestic courts the power to disapply provisions of the TCA. Option E is incorrect because Parliament cannot simply overrule aspects of the TCA.

Did you choose the correct answer?   YES ☐   NO ☐

See *Revise SQE: Constitutional and Administrative Law*, **Chapter 9** for a discussion of this area of law.

A84 of 90 (page 43)   **Area of law assessed: Constitutional and administrative law and EU law**

The correct answer was A. This is because the police have the power to impose conditions on protestors (ie, instruct the protestors to move their demonstration) where there is a reasonable belief that the demonstration may result in serious disorder (option D is therefore incorrect). Option B is incorrect because the police may impose conditions before a public order offence has been committed, providing there is a reasonable belief that the demonstration may result in serious disorder. Option C is incorrect because it misstates the threshold for imposing a condition. Option E is incorrect because notice of such conditions does not need to be given in advance of the protest.

Did you choose the correct answer?   YES ☐   NO ☐

See *Revise SQE: Constitutional and Administrative Law*, **Chapter 6** for a discussion of this area of law.

A85 of 90 (page 43)   **Area of law assessed: Tort law**

The correct answer was D. This is because an acceptance of risk by a passenger is invalid; this means that the defence of consent would fail. Option A is incorrect because a passenger is unable to consent as their consent to the risk is invalid. Option B is incorrect because the court would only consider contributory negligence once primary liability had been established and this will not be the case here. Option C is incorrect because the claimant is unable to consent to the risk even though the accident is caused by the defendant's negligence. Option E is incorrect because even though the defendant is deceased, a claim in negligence could be brought against the defendant's estate.

Did you choose the correct answer?   YES ☐   NO ☐

See *Revise SQE: Tort Law*, **Chapter 4** for a discussion of this area of law.

A86 of 90 (page 44)   **Area of law assessed: Dispute resolution**

The correct answer was C. This is because a reply to the defence would not be appropriate here as this would simply allow the defence, which on the face of it is wholly lacking in substance, to continue (making option A incorrect). An application for default judgment would only be applicable if the defendant had failed to either acknowledge service or defend the claim, which is not the case here (therefore options D and E are incorrect). To be successful in an application for default judgment, the claimant must prove that the defendant has no real prospect of successfully defending the claim *and* that there is no compelling reason why the claim should proceed to trial (therefore, option B is incorrect).

Did you choose the correct answer?   YES ☐   NO ☐

See *Revise SQE: Dispute Resolution*, **Chapter 6** for a discussion of this area of law.

A87 of 90 (page 44)   **Area of law assessed: Legal services**

The correct answer was B. This is because the solicitor is acting in the sale of the shares in order to wind up the estate and allow the executors to make a distribution. This type of work is permissible because an exclusion from the general prohibition would apply. Options A and C are incorrect because the solicitor may only engage in such activities where an exclusion applies. Option D is incorrect because legal service providers are not classified as authorised persons under financial services legislation. Option E is incorrect because it fails to acknowledge that the nature of the solicitor's work would be covered by an exclusion.

Did you choose the correct answer?   YES ☐   NO ☐

See *Revise SQE: The Legal System and Services of England and Wales*, **Chapter 7** for a discussion of this area of law.

A88 of 90 (page 45)   **Area of law assessed: Dispute resolution**

The correct answer was A. This is because if the court is persuaded at the hearing that the defendant has even slightly more than a fanciful chance of successfully defending the claim, rather than dismiss the application outright (making option D incorrect) or giving judgment on the claim (making options B and C incorrect), they will make a conditional order requiring the defendant to file a proper defence setting out their legal and factual position within 14 days of the date of the hearing (therefore option E is incorrect).

Did you choose the correct answer?   YES ☐   NO ☐

See *Revise SQE: Dispute Resolution*, **Chapter 6** for a discussion of this area of law.

A89 of 90 (page 45)   **Area of law assessed: Contract law**

The correct answer was C. This is because the loss appears to be normal loss resulting from the breach of contract. As such, this loss will be recoverable as it would be reasonably contemplated by the manufacturer. However, this is subject to the general duty of the business to take reasonable steps to mitigate its loss. As a replacement generator was available, the court may decide to reduce the award appropriately in light of any failure of the business to mitigate its loss. Option A is incorrect as it recognises the general test of remoteness, but it does not mention the general duty of mitigation. Option B is incorrect as whilst it shows an awareness of the test of remoteness of damage, it fails to recognise that the business could have taken reasonable steps to mitigate their loss. Option D is incorrect as this is a general statement about the measure of damage for breach of contract. It does not reference the test of remoteness or the duty to mitigate. Option E is incorrect as the test of *reasonable foreseeability* is the test of remoteness in the law of tort (see *Revise SQE: Tort Law*), which is not the appropriate test in a claim for breach of contract.

Did you choose the correct answer?   YES ☐   NO ☐

See *Revise SQE: Contract Law*, **Chapter 10** for a discussion of this area of law.

A90 of 90 (page 46)   **Area of law assessed: Ethics and professional conduct**

The correct answer was C. This is because the SRA Code of Conduct requires solicitors to ensure that they do not mislead or attempt to mislead their clients, the court or others, either by their own acts or omissions or allowing or being complicit in the acts or omissions of others (including their client). If the solicitor were to allow the evidence of the medical expert witness to go unchanged, the solicitor would be misleading the court (therefore option A is incorrect). Option B is incorrect as whilst it is appropriate to speak to the expert and advise them that their evidence was exaggerated, that does not resolve the situation faced by the solicitor: they would still be misleading the court if they did not correct the position. Option D is incorrect as it does not resolve the issue that the court in the current proceedings has been misled. Whilst option E is correct, in that the medical expert witness should be asked to provide a more accurate assessment of the injuries, the court must first be informed that the original evidence was exaggerated. Otherwise, the court would have still been misled.

Did you choose the correct answer?   YES ☐   NO ☐

See *Revise SQE: Ethics and Professional Conduct*, **Chapter 2** for a discussion of this area of law.

Session 2 answers

■ SUMMARY

The following table is a quick reference guide for the answers to Session 2 of *Prepare for SQE1: FLK1 Practice Assessment*. Consider using a coloured pen or a highlighter to mark the MCQs that you answered correctly, and score yourself 1 mark for each. Add up your total marks, and calculate your percentage for Session 2.

For a summary of the Session 1 answers, see **page 94**.

Question	Answer	Question	Answer	Question	Answer
1	C	31	C	61	D
2	E	32	D	62	B
3	E	33	B	63	D
4	D	34	A	64	C
5	D	35	C	65	E
6	B	36	E	66	D
7	B	37	B	67	D
8	B	38	C	68	D
9	E	39	B	69	C
10	E	40	B	70	D
11	D	41	B	71	B
12	A	42	D	72	D
13	E	43	D	73	B
14	D	44	C	74	B
15	B	45	D	75	A
16	A	46	E	76	E
17	C	47	A	77	D
18	B	48	D	78	C
19	E	49	A	79	A
20	B	50	A	80	E
21	E	51	B	81	B
22	C	52	B	82	C
23	A	53	D	83	E
24	A	54	A	84	A
25	B	55	D	85	B
26	B	56	E	86	A
27	A	57	D	87	D
28	C	58	D	88	B
29	E	59	A	89	B
30	E	60	C	90	D

Your total score for Session 2: _____ / 90

Percentage: _____ %

■ DETAILED ANSWERS

A1 of 90 (page 48)   **Area of law assessed: Dispute resolution**

The correct answer was C. This is because the value in dispute is actually £9,000 once the interest and the amount admitted are taken into consideration, which makes the claim suitable for the small claims track (therefore, options A and B are incorrect). The court considers value primarily when allocating a claim, making C the best answer and ruling out options D and E.

Did you choose the correct answer?   YES ☐   NO ☐

See *Revise SQE: Dispute Resolution*, **Chapter 7** for a discussion of this area of law.

A2 of 90 (page 48)   **Area of law assessed: Legal services**

The correct answer was E. Specified investments are defined in financial services legislation. The legislation lists shares and gilts as specified investments. Investment property is not classified as a specified investment under the legislation. Options A, B, C and D are incorrect because they do not accurately identify which of the assets are classified as specified investments under financial services legislation.

Did you choose the correct answer?   YES ☐   NO ☐

See *Revise SQE: The Legal System and Services of England and Wales*, **Chapter 7** for a discussion of this area of law.

A3 of 90 (page 49)   **Area of law assessed: Business law and practice**

The correct answer was E. This is because, whilst options A, B and C will happen in order to ensure transfer of the beneficial ownership of the shares and comply with company law, they are not essential to the transfer of legal ownership. Option D should of course happen but is not essential here.

Did you choose the correct answer?   YES ☐   NO ☐

See *Revise SQE: Business Law and Practice*, **Chapter 3** for a discussion of this area of law.

A4 of 90 (page 49)   **Area of law assessed: Contract law**

The correct answer was D. This is because the remedy of rescission is an equitable remedy and is subject to several bars. If upon discovering the truth of the misrepresentation, the claimant acts so as to accept the misrepresentation, the court is likely to determine that the contract is affirmed and the claimant will be barred from claiming rescission. By running the promotional campaign and lowering prices, the buyer is likely to have affirmed the contract. Option A is incorrect as rescission is generally available for all types of mispresenting, providing that the elements of an actionable misrepresentation are established. The question requires you to respond on the basis that the claim for misrepresentation is successful. The statement must have induced the contract in order for the statement to be actionable and for the claim to be successful (therefore, option B is incorrect). Option C is a broadly correct statement, but it does not recognise that rescission is at the court's discretion, subject to a number of bars (it is therefore incorrect). It is true that a lapse of time may bar a claim for rescission. However, a lapse of time of over six months from the seller discovering the truth of the misrepresentation is unlikely to be reasonable. It also does not take account of any affirmation by the buyer (option E is therefore incorrect).

Did you choose the correct answer?   YES ☐   NO ☐

See *Revise SQE: Contract Law*, **Chapter 10** for a discussion of this area of law.

A5 of 90 (page 50)   **Area of law assessed: Legal system of England and Wales and sources of law**

The correct answer was D. This is because the Court of Appeal distinguished itself from the Supreme Court. This means the Court of Appeal did not apply the Supreme Court authority because it believed the case facts were materially different from those of the instant case. The Supreme Court's decision remains a precedent which is binding of all inferior courts (options B, C and E are therefore incorrect). Option A is incorrect because it implies that inferior courts may choose not to apply the Supreme Court authority, which is not accurate.

Did you choose the correct answer?   YES ☐   NO ☐

See *Revise SQE: The Legal System and Services of England and Wales*, **Chapter 4** for a discussion of this area of law.

A6 of 90 (page 50)   **Area of law assessed: Contract law**

The correct answer was B. This is because only a false statement of fact that induces the contract will give rise to an actionable misrepresentation. Option A is incorrect as it is not a requirement of an actionable misrepresentation, in the law of contract, that a statement was made fraudulently. This statement also fails to identify that only a false statement of fact can give rise to an actionable misrepresentation. Option C is incorrect as a statement of opinion is generally not actionable for misrepresentation in the law of contract. Option D is incorrect as this statement fails to identify that only a false statement of fact, not opinion, will give rise to an actionable misrepresentation in the law of contract. Option E is incorrect as an opportunity to discover the truth or verify the statement will not generally release the maker of the statement from liability. The statement also fails to identify that the false statement must be one of fact to be actionable.

Did you choose the correct answer?   YES ☐   NO ☐

See *Revise SQE: Contract Law*, **Chapter 9** for a discussion of this area of law.

A7 of 90 (page 51)   **Area of law assessed: Ethics and professional conduct**

The correct answer was B. This is because the SRA Code of Conduct requires solicitors not to waste the court's time. By providing a lengthy and irrelevant answer, the solicitor has already wasted the court's time. Option A is incorrect as the solicitor would continue to waste the court's time should they adopt that approach. Option C is incorrect as the solicitor would also be misleading the court by providing an answer that they know to be incorrect. Whilst option D is correct, in that the solicitor should be honest with the District Judge, the solicitor is best advised to seek a short adjournment to ensure that the court is aware of the correct position and to ensure that the solicitor acts in the best interests of the client. Option E is incorrect as the solicitor would not be acting in the best interests of the client by ceasing to act.

Did you choose the correct answer?   YES ☐   NO ☐

See *Revise SQE: Ethics and Professional Conduct*, **Chapter 2** for a discussion of this area of law.

A8 of 90 (page 51)   **Area of law assessed: Legal system of England and Wales and sources of law**

The correct answer was B. This is because statutes that include a specific commencement date come into effect on the date specified in the commencement provision. In some cases, the commencement provision only brings specific parts of the Act into effect because some sections have a commencement date that is 'yet to be appointed' and those provisions must be brought into effect through a statutory instrument. The information provided states that the commencement date for section 1 of the Act is 'yet to be appointed'. This means that section 1 will come into effect when a statutory instrument has been enacted to bring it into effect. Statutes that do not include a commencement provision usually come into effect on the date the Act received Royal Assent. The Act includes a commencement provision that determines how and when the Act comes into effect (therefore, options A and C are incorrect). The enacting formula does not impact when or how an Act of Parliament comes into effect (therefore, option D is incorrect). Option E is incorrect because it states that the whole Act comes into effect on the commencement date. The enacting formula is a short paragraph of text, which precedes the main provisions in the statute.

Did you choose the correct answer?   YES ☐   NO ☐

See *Revise SQE: The Legal System and Services of England and Wales*, **Chapter 2** for a discussion of this area of law.

A9 of 90 (page 52)   Area of law assessed: Tort law

The correct answer was E. This is because there is a connection between the defendant's actions and the claimant's injuries, and it would be adverse to public policy to allow the claimant to be awarded damages for their injuries. Option A is incorrect because the claimant did not consent to their injuries. Option B is incorrect because although the injuries are caused by the defendant's negligence, it is contrary to public policy to allow the claimant to succeed in an action for personal injury. Option C is incorrect because the claimant's injuries are directly connected to the defendant's actions. Option D is incorrect because in order for contributory negligence to attach, the defendant would have to be found primarily liable and this is not the case here.

Did you choose the correct answer?   YES ☐   NO ☐

See *Revise SQE: Tort Law*, **Chapter 4** for a discussion of this area of law.

A10 of 90 (page 52)   Area of law assessed: Contract law

The correct answer was E. This is because the facts are likely to amount to economic duress being applied by the haulage company to the supplier. In such cases, the courts will not enforce an otherwise apparently enforceable agreement that has been induced by duress. The timing of the haulage company's threat to the breach of contract left the supplier with no time to find an alternative haulage company. Damages are unlikely to be an adequate remedy, as the loss of the ongoing relationship with the retail customer (the supplier's biggest customer) could far outweigh the amount the supplier may recover in damages. We are also told that the supplier could not recover such a loss, again meaning that enforcing their rights under the contract and claiming damages may not be realistic for the supplier. The performance of an existing contractual duty may constitute good consideration if it confers a practical benefit to the promisor. However, such a principle will not apply when the promise of an additional amount has been induced by duress or fraud (therefore option A is incorrect). Option B is incorrect because the recognition of consideration constituting some practical benefit will not apply when the promise of an additional amount has been induced by duress. Option C is incorrect because any disbenefit avoided will not constitute good consideration due to economic duress. As noted above, given the importance of the ongoing relationship between the supplier and the retail customer, it is unlikely that damages will provide an adequate remedy (option D is therefore incorrect).

Did you choose the correct answer?   YES ☐   NO ☐

See *Revise SQE: Contract Law*, **Chapter 2** for a discussion of this area of law.

A11 of 90 (page 53)   **Area of law assessed: Tort law**

The correct answer was D. This is because the duty to provide a safe system of work cannot be delegated regardless of where an employee works. This means that the claimant's employer should have assessed the premises where their employees were sent, to ensure that a safe system of work was implemented. Option A is incorrect because an employer has to assess premises where employees are sent, to minimise any dangers and implement a safe system of work. Option B is incorrect as the employer owes a duty to the employee which cannot be delegated to the ferry company. Option C is incorrect as, if the premises are unsafe, there is a foreseeable risk of injury to employees. Option E is incorrect as an employer cannot delegate their duties in the circumstances.

Did you choose the correct answer?   YES ☐   NO ☐

See *Revise SQE: Tort Law*, **Chapter 5** for a discussion of this area of law.

A12 of 90 (page 53)   **Area of law assessed: Ethics and professional conduct**

The correct answer was A. This is because the SRA Code of Conduct requires a solicitor to properly account to clients for any financial benefit they receive as a result of their instructions, except where they have agreed otherwise. This includes referral fees for introducing clients to third-party services. The solicitor must notify the client of the referral fees and is only permitted to receive those fees with the consent of the client. If the client does not consent, the solicitor is not permitted to receive those fees (therefore option D is incorrect). Options B, C and E are incorrect as the solicitor must inform the client of the referral fees; the reasons given are not valid under the Code of Conduct.

Did you choose the correct answer?   YES ☐   NO ☐

See *Revise SQE: Ethics and Professional Conduct*, **Chapter 2** for a discussion of this area of law.

A13 of 90 (page 54)   **Area of law assessed: Legal services**

The correct answer was E. This is because anti-money laundering legislation requires firms to follow standard customer due diligence when it forms a new business relationship with a client. Option A is incorrect because other forms of identification are acceptable under the legislation. The duty to carry out standard customer due diligence may also arise where a firm is carrying out an occasional transaction. However, options B and D are incorrect because the relevant threshold for an occasional transaction would be around £15,000. Option C is incorrect because there is no need for the firm to follow enhanced due diligence in this scenario.

Did you choose the correct answer?   YES ☐   NO ☐

See *Revise SQE: The Legal System and Services of England and Wales*, **Chapter 6** for a discussion of this area of law.

A14 of 90 (page 54)   **Area of law assessed: Business law and practice**

The correct answer was D. This is because option D represents the correct procedure for the removal of a director. Options A, C and E are legally incorrect: option A is incorrect as the process of appointing a director is not the same as that to remove a director. Option C is incorrect as only an ordinary resolution is required to remove a director. Option E is incorrect, as a director cannot be automatically removed following termination of his service contract. Option B is incorrect as, whilst it may need to be considered in a particular case, there is no evidence on these facts that there is any weighted voting clause.

Did you choose the correct answer?   YES ☐   NO ☐

See *Revise SQE: Business Law and Practice*, **Chapter 4** for a discussion of this area of law.

A15 of 90 (page 55)   Area of law assessed: Constitutional and administrative law and EU law

The correct answer was B. This is because Parliament may give the Secretary of State a specific power to introduce such regulations (option D is therefore incorrect). Parliament must give the Secretary of State its power to make such regulations through an enabling or parent Act (options A and E are therefore incorrect). Option C is incorrect because it implies the Secretary of State could introduce such regulations irrespective of whether an enabling or parent Act gives such power to the Secretary of State.

Did you choose the correct answer?   YES ☐   NO ☐

See *Revise SQE: Constitutional and Administrative Law*, **Chapter 5** for a discussion of this area of law.

A16 of 90 (page 55)   Area of law assessed: Tort law

The correct answer was A. This is because in order for a warning to defeat a claim for negligence, the warning should be sufficient enough to ensure the visitor would be reasonably safe. In this case, the warning signs should have referred to the uneven floorboards in the corridor. Option B is incorrect because the warning is not sufficiently specific to provide a defence to the claim. Option C is incorrect as the claimant was not a trespasser but a visitor to the premises. Option D is incorrect as an incidental breach refers to a situation where the visitor can be expected to safeguard themselves against a risk. Option E is incorrect as the warning sign is not specific enough and the court is unlikely to find that the claimant contributed to their injuries in the circumstances.

Did you choose the correct answer?   YES ☐   NO ☐

See *Revise SQE: Tort Law*, **Chapter 6** for a discussion of this area of law.

A17 of 90 (page 56)   Area of law assessed: Contract law

The correct answer was C. This is because whilst £1 per year may not be adequate in terms of how it relates to the market value of the property, it will be legally sufficient. Consideration provides the general test of enforceability of promises at common law. Reliance in and of itself does not make a promise binding at common law (therefore, option A is incorrect). Option B is incorrect because the courts are not generally concerned with the adequacy of consideration (how it relates in value to what is bargained for), providing consideration is legally sufficient. Providing consideration has *some* economic value, however small, it will generally constitute sufficient consideration (therefore, option D is incorrect). The woman is giving her promise of £1 per year in exchange for the executor's promise. This is therefore not an example of past consideration (option E is therefore incorrect).

Did you choose the correct answer?   YES ☐   NO ☐

See *Revise SQE: Contract Law*, **Chapter 2** for a discussion of this area of law.

A18 of 90 (page 56)   **Area of law assessed: Business law and practice**

The correct answer was B. This is because Business Asset Rollover Relief, if the brothers elect to use it, has the effect of postponing any liability to Capital Gains Tax because any gain will be added to any future gain and tax will be payable when the premises are eventually sold. Option A, whilst it is technically correct, is unlikely to be true here because the brothers are unlikely to want to pay tax before they have to. Option C is incorrect as it presents an out-of-date annual exempt amount figure. Option D is only applicable to transactions at an undervalue/gifts. Option E is incorrect as the use of Business Asset Rollover Relief does not extinguish liability to pay Capital Gains Tax – it postpones it.

Did you choose the correct answer?   YES ☐   NO ☐

See *Revise SQE: Business Law and Practice*, **Chapter 9** for a discussion of this area of law.

A19 of 90 (page 57)   **Area of law assessed: Legal system of England and Wales and sources of law**

The correct answer was E. This is because the Supreme Court has *reversed* the decision of the Court of Appeal (Civil Division). This means that the Court of Appeal decision is no longer considered to be good law and it is not binding on any inferior court (option A is therefore incorrect). It is important to remember the difference between a court *overturning* a decision and a court *reversing* a decision. Here, the Supreme Court considered the Court of Appeal's decision on appeal. This means that it has reversed, rather than overruled or overturned, the Court of Appeal decision (options B and D are therefore incorrect). Option C is incorrect because it states that the Supreme Court has distinguished the Court of Appeal decision.

Did you choose the correct answer?   YES ☐   NO ☐

See *Revise SQE: The Legal System and Services of England and Wales*, **Chapter 4** for a discussion of this area of law.

A20 of 90 (page 57)   **Area of law assessed: Tort law**

The correct answer was B. This is because business occupiers are unable to exclude or restrict their liability for personal injury or death. Option A is incorrect as the exclusion of liability notice is invalid. Option C is incorrect as the injury caused to the claimant is foreseeable if the lift doors are defective. Option D is incorrect as business occupiers are unable to exclude or restrict liability for negligence to non-consumers, and the hotel did owe the claimant as a visitor a duty of care. Option E is incorrect as the claimant's injuries have been caused by the state of the premises.

Did you choose the correct answer?   YES ☐   NO ☐

See *Revise SQE: Tort Law*, **Chapter 6** for a discussion of this area of law.

A21 of 90 (page 58)   **Area of law assessed: Contract law**

The correct answer was E. This is because a doctor–patient relationship is a recognised relationship from which influence is to be presumed. A presumption of influence will arise when the parties in such a relationship enter into a transaction that 'calls for explanation'. The sale of the house so far under market value, from a patient to their doctor, is one that calls for explanation. The woman must then establish that she did not apply such influence to the man in order to avoid a finding of undue influence. Option A was incorrect because the statement does not address the issue of undue influence as stated in the question. There would be no need for the man to prove actual undue influence, as the relationship is one from which influence would be presumed. Further, there is no overt evidence of this on the facts (therefore, option B is incorrect). Option C is incorrect because the burden of establishing undue influence would not fall on the man due to the nature of his relationship with the woman. Option D is incorrect because the relationship is a recognised relationship of trust and confidence. Even this on its own is not enough to raise a presumption of influence. There must also be a transaction that calls for explanation.

Did you choose the correct answer?   YES ☐   NO ☐

See *Revise SQE: Contract Law*, **Chapter 8** for a discussion of this area of law.

A22 of 90 (page 58)   Area of law assessed: Dispute resolution

The correct answer was C. This is because, whilst the overriding objective states that cases must be dealt with fairly and seek, where possible, to put parties on an equal footing, this is always with proportionality in mind (therefore options A and B are incorrect). Similarly, whilst reference is made to the need to ensure that cases are allotted an appropriate share of the court's resources, this is not the primary reason the two expert reports and the volume of emails will not be allowed (making option D incorrect). The primary reason will be that the volume of evidence is disproportionate to the value of the claim (therefore option E is incorrect).

Did you choose the correct answer?   YES ☐   NO ☐

See *Revise SQE: Dispute Resolution*, **Chapter 7** for a discussion of this area of law.

A23 of 90 (page 59)   Area of law assessed: Constitutional and administrative law and EU law

The correct answer was A. This is because the UK is no longer a member of the European Union so any EU law made after exit day (31 January 2020) has no effect in UK law. Options B, C, D and E are therefore incorrect.

Did you choose the correct answer?   YES ☐   NO ☐

See *Revise SQE: Constitutional and Administrative Law*, **Chapter 9** for a discussion of this area of law.

A24 of 90 (page 59)   Area of law assessed: Constitutional and administrative law and EU law

The correct answer was A. This is because applications for judicial review must be submitted to the Administrative Court and must be filed no later than three months from the date on which the grounds to make a claim first arose. Additionally, the claimant must be able to demonstrate that the claim is arguable and has a reasonable prospect of success. Options D and E are incorrect because they state that the claimant must demonstrate a *good* prospect of success when the correct threshold is a *reasonable* prospect of success. Option C is incorrect because it states that applications for judicial review must be made within six weeks. This deadline would only apply to judicial review of planning claims, so would not apply here. Options B and D are incorrect because they state that judicial review applications must be submitted to the Court of Appeal. All applications for judicial review must be submitted to the Administrative Court.

Did you choose the correct answer?   YES ☐   NO ☐

See *Revise SQE: Constitutional and Administrative Law*, **Chapter 7** for a discussion of this area of law.

A25 of 90 (page 60)   **Area of law assessed: Contract law**

The correct answer was B. This is because a clause that seeks to protect a legitimate interest of the employer must be reasonable. From the facts of the question, there is no evidence as to why a wholesale restriction, for such a long period, is reasonably necessary on the facts. Option A is incorrect because a restriction preventing the man from working as a salesperson in any industry is not reasonably established on the facts. Option C is incorrect as there are limits to the principle of freedom of contract, and a contract in restraint of trade may be unenforceable at common law if it does not reasonably protect a legitimate interest of the employer. A reasonable restriction in order to protect a legitimate interest of the employer may be binding, so it is not true to say that all clauses in restraint of trade are unenforceable (therefore, option D is incorrect). Option E is incorrect because there is no evidence on the facts that the clause seeks to protect the trade secrets of the employer.

Did you choose the correct answer?   YES ☐   NO ☐

See *Revise SQE: Contract Law*, **Chapter 8** for a discussion of this area of law.

A26 of 90 (page 60)   **Area of law assessed: Ethics and professional conduct**

The correct answer was B. The is because the SRA Code of Conduct requires a solicitor to identify who they are acting for in relation to any matter. Generally, the client will be asked to attend the firm with two forms of identification and relevant financial statements. The solicitor must check this identification as part of their due diligence and anti-money laundering checks. The solicitor must not accept the oral representations from the client or assume that the client is who they identify themselves as being (therefore option A is incorrect). Option C is incorrect because the first meeting is irrelevant if the client has retained the solicitor. Option D is incorrect as the solicitor has a personal responsibility to identify who they are acting for; relying on information from the partner is not appropriate (therefore option E is also incorrect).

Did you choose the correct answer?   YES ☐   NO ☐

See *Revise SQE: Ethics and Professional Conduct*, **Chapter 2** for a discussion of this area of law.

A27 of 90 (page 61)   **Area of law assessed: Business law and practice**

The correct answer was A. This is because option A is not an option available to the client. Only a shareholder owning more than 5% of the shares has the right to ask the directors to call an extraordinary general meeting. All of the other options are available (even if not desirable) and are thus incorrect answers.

Did you choose the correct answer?   YES ☐   NO ☐

See *Revise SQE: Business Law and Practice*, **Chapter 4** for a discussion of this area of law.

A28 of 90 (page 61)   **Area of law assessed: Dispute resolution**

The correct answer was C. This is because, whilst there is no good reason for the failure to comply (making options D and E incorrect), a 45-minute delay is likely to be found to be trivial and the breach did not impact on any future court hearings. Option A is incorrect because, whilst the court's role is to enforce compliance, the failure is so minor that the court would be unlikely to reject the application. However, given the breach was the fault of the egal representative, it is likely that a wasted costs order would be made against the solicitor for breaching the deadline, as opposed to requiring the claimant to pay the parties' costs (therefore option B is incorrect).

Did you choose the correct answer?   YES ☐   NO ☐

See *Revise SQE: Dispute Resolution*, **Chapter 7** for a discussion of this area of law.

A29 of 90 (page 62)   **Area of law assessed: Ethics and professional conduct**

The correct answer was E. The is because the SRA Code of Conduct requires a solicitor to report promptly to the SRA or another approved regulator, as appropriate, any facts or matters that they reasonably believe are capable of amounting to a serious breach of their regulatory arrangements by any person regulated by them (including themselves). Furthermore, the Code of Conduct requires that the solicitor does not subject any person to detrimental treatment for making or proposing to make a report or providing or proposing to provide information based on such a reasonably held belief. Option A is incorrect as the solicitor should not be seeking to prevent someone from reporting a matter to the SRA. Options B, C and D are incorrect as it would not be appropriate in this circumstance to speak to the senior partner about their own conduct; a report is to be made to the SRA.

Did you choose the correct answer?   YES ☐   NO ☐

See *Revise SQE: Ethics and Professional Conduct*, **Chapter 2** for a discussion of this area of law.

A30 of 90 (page 62)   **Area of law assessed: Legal services**

The correct answer was E. This is because under financial services legislation, only specific advice concerning specified investments is prohibited. In this scenario, the advice provided by the solicitor is generic (options B and D are therefore incorrect). Furthermore, the advice provided does not relate to a specified investment because land is not a specified investment under financial services legislation (option A is therefore incorrect as it does not explain that land is not a specified investment). Option C is incorrect because the solicitor's advice was not given in the course of a wider legal service as the client's claim has concluded.

Did you choose the correct answer?   YES ☐   NO ☐

See *Revise SQE: The Legal System and Services of England and Wales*, **Chapter 7** for a discussion of this area of law.

A31 of 90 (page 63)   **Area of law assessed: Legal services**

The correct answer was C. This is because the Damages Based Agreement (DBA) is set at 10% of the damages awarded. The client's case was successful, so the solicitor is entitled to 10% of the damages awarded (10% of £55,000). The solicitor is therefore owed £5,500. The other party is liable to pay £1,000 which leaves the client with a shortfall of £4,500. This will be deducted from the damages and the client will receive the remaining £50,500. All other options are therefore incorrect.

Did you choose the correct answer?   YES ☐   NO ☐

See *Revise SQE: The Legal System and Services of England and Wales*, **Chapter 8** for a discussion of this area of law.

A32 of 90 (page 63)   **Area of law assessed: Dispute resolution**

The correct answer was D. This is because the Civil Procedure Rules 1998 lays out the formalities that a witness statement needs to comply with. This MCQ specifically asks which option should be *omitted*. The necessity for a statement of truth is paramount to a witness statement (therefore, option A is incorrect). Witness statements should also be expressed in the witness's own words where possible (therefore option B is incorrect), indicate which statements are from their own knowledge (making option E incorrect) and only include evidence that they would be allowed to make in an oral submission (making option C incorrect).

Did you choose the correct answer?   YES ☐   NO ☐

See *Revise SQE: Dispute Resolution*, **Chapter 8** for a discussion of this area of law.

A33 of 90 (page 64)   **Area of law assessed: Legal system of England and Wales and sources of law**

The correct answer was B. This is because the Court of Appeal is bound to follow the decisions of any court above it in the court hierarchy. The House of Lords (which has now been replaced by the Supreme Court) was above the Court of Appeal in the court hierarchy. House of Lords decisions continue to bind lower courts despite being replaced by the Supreme Court. This means that the previous decision of the House of Lords remains binding on the Court of Appeal (option D is therefore incorrect). Remember that the passing of time does not impact whether a binding precedent binds a lower court. Option C is therefore incorrect. There are limited circumstances in which the Court of Appeal may depart from its own decisions. However, these circumstances do not apply to this scenario because the Court of Appeal is bound by the House of Lords decision in any event (options A and E are therefore incorrect).

Did you choose the correct answer?   YES ☐   NO ☐

See *Revise SQE: The Legal System and Services of England and Wales*, **Chapter 4** for a discussion of this area of law.

A34 of 90 (page 64)   **Area of law assessed: Contract law**

The correct answer was A. This is because various breaches could result in the vessel being unfit for ordinary cargo service. In this scenario, it is difficult to anticipate the various ways in which the breach could occur, and the seriousness of the breach. As such, it is likely that the courts would construe the term as an innominate term. The breach is relatively minor and does not deprive the shipping company of the entire value of the contract as the vessel can be used for the remainder of the charter. It is likely that this breach will be treated as a breach of warranty. Damages would provide an adequate remedy for the three-month delay and the breach would not repudiate the agreement. Given the relatively minor breach, and that the vessel can be used for the rest of the period of the charter, it is unlikely that the beach will be considered as a breach of condition (therefore option B is incorrect). If the breach is construed as a breach of warranty, then the shipping company has no right to repudiate the agreement (option C is therefore incorrect). Option D was incorrect as the owners of the vessel would be strictly liable for breach of the term. The key issue is whether this repudiates the agreement, or simply gives rise to a claim for damages, as noted above. The inadequate safety equipment and the three-month delay do not radically alter the obligations or make the contract impossible to perform. It is very unlikely that the contract is frustrated on the facts (therefore option E is incorrect).

Did you choose the correct answer?   YES ☐   NO ☐

See *Revise SQE: Contract Law*, **Chapter 9** for a discussion of this area of law.

A35 of 90 (page 65)   **Area of law assessed: Tort law**

The correct answer was C. This is because the owners of the retail outlet have a defence on the basis that it was reasonable to employ an independent contractor and that the independent contractor was reputable and competent to undertake the rewiring of the retail outlet. Option A is incorrect as the claimant cannot consent to the risk of injury as they were unaware that there was a risk of injury. Option B is incorrect: as long as the retail outlet have satisfied themselves that they have employed competent contractors, they will have a defence to the claim. Option D is incorrect as the retail outlet has a duty to ensure their visitors are safe, but if they have contracted the rewiring of the retail outlet to a competent contractor, the claim against them will not succeed. Option E is incorrect as there was a foreseeable risk of injury on the basis that there was a problem with the wiring at the retail outlet.

Did you choose the correct answer?   YES ☐   NO ☐

See *Revise SQE: Tort Law*, **Chapter 6** for a discussion of this area of law.

A36 of 90 (page 65)   **Area of law assessed: Tort law**

The correct answer was E. This is because all those injured are consumers for the purpose of negligence in respect of the defective product (the engine). Therefore, all other options are incorrect on the basis that anyone injured due to the defective engine will be deemed to be a consumer for the purposes of defective product liability.

Did you choose the correct answer?   YES ☐   NO ☐

See *Revise SQE: Tort Law*, **Chapter 7** for a discussion of this area of law.

A37 of 90 (page 66)   **Area of law assessed: Legal system of England and Wales and sources of law**

The correct answer was B. This is because civil claims that are valued at less than £100,000 should usually be commenced in the County Court. Cases valued at less than £100,000 may be commenced in the High Court if they are particularly complex. The facts here make clear that the case is relatively straightforward so there is no reason to commence this claim in the High Court (options A and C are therefore incorrect). In personal injury cases, claims valued above £50,000 may be commenced in the High Court. The claim in this scenario relates to a breach of contract so the £50,000 threshold is not relevant (therefore options D and E are incorrect).

Did you choose the correct answer?   YES ☐   NO ☐

See *Revise SQE: The Legal System and Services of England and Wales*, **Chapter 1** for a discussion of this area of law.

A38 of 90 (page 66)   **Area of law assessed: Tort law**

The correct answer was C. This is because damage to business property (the work laptop and the work smartphone) is outside the scope of the Consumer Protection Act 1987 and damage to personal property (the personal computer and personal smartphone) must exceed £275 in value. Options A and D are incorrect due to the business property exclusion under the Act. Option B is incorrect as the claim for damage to personal property will succeed (if the value exceeds £275). Option E is incorrect as damage to the charger is economic loss and this is not covered under the Act.

Did you choose the correct answer?   YES ☐   NO ☐

See *Revise SQE: Tort Law*, **Chapter 7** for a discussion of this area of law.

A39 of 90 (page 67)   **Area of law assessed: Business law and practice**

The correct answer was B. This is because all elements of the option are correct. Option A is incorrect because Shareholder A with 50% cannot pass an ordinary resolution, but can block one. Option C is incorrect as Shareholder B has insufficient shares to block a special resolution. Option D is incorrect as Shareholder B is a person of significant control, whereas option E is incorrect as Shareholder C is not a person of significant control.

Did you choose the correct answer?   YES ☐   NO ☐

See *Revise SQE: Business Law and Practice*, **Chapter 4** for a discussion of this area of law.

A40 of 90 (page 67)   **Area of law assessed: Dispute resolution**

The correct answer was B. This is because although there is not quite enough in the defence to demonstrate that the defendant has a real prospect of successfully defending the claim (making option C incorrect), the court will almost certainly need to hear oral evidence from other witnesses to establish whether time was of the essence and will need to take place at trial. This would therefore be a compelling reason why the claim should proceed to trial (therefore, option D is incorrect). The defendant's defence provides sufficient detail for the court to see there is an issue that needs to be tried (making option A incorrect) and it is very unlikely that the court would make a conditional order in these circumstances (therefore, option E is incorrect).

Did you choose the correct answer?   YES ☐   NO ☐

See *Revise SQE: Dispute Resolution*, **Chapter 7** for a discussion of this area of law.

A41 of 90 (page 68)   **Area of law assessed: Dispute resolution**

The correct answer was B. This is because the court will look at the basis on which costs have been awarded; the standard basis. This means that the court must take proportionality into consideration when making its award (therefore options C, D and E are incorrect). With the value of the claim being £475,000, the claimant's claim for £345,000 is therefore likely to be viewed as being disproportionate and the trial judge will consider each item in the cost breakdown to see whether it was reasonably incurred (and if not, it will be disallowed) and reasonable in amount (and if not, it will be reduced). With the claim being a multi-track high-value matter, the parties have already submitted and had approved a costs budget, which the trial judge must take into consideration. Proportionality of the costs budget is also considered by the judge in the directions hearing, and so it is highly likely that the claimant will recover the costs that were submitted as part of the costs budget but not the full value they have claimed (therefore option A is incorrect).

Did you choose the correct answer?   YES ☐   NO ☐

See *Revise SQE: Dispute Resolution*, **Chapter 10** for a discussion of this area of law.

A42 of 90 (page 68)   **Area of law assessed: Business law and practice**

The correct answer was D. This is because the client appears to be describing a limited liability partnership (LLP). An LLP has a separate legal personality, unlike a traditional partnership therefore option A is incorrect). The main distinction between an LLP and a company is that shareholders in any of the companies described in options B, C and E cannot be removed by a majority of others.

Did you choose the correct answer?   YES ☐   NO ☐

See *Revise SQE: Business Law and Practice*, **Chapter 1** for a discussion of this area of law.

A43 of 90 (page 69)   **Area of law assessed: Constitutional and administrative law and EU law**

The correct answer was D. This is because the man is likely to be deemed to have sufficient interest in the claim. Option A is incorrect because there is no requirement for a claimant to demonstrate that a significant proportion of the public have been impacted by the local authority's decision. The man only needs to be able to demonstrate that his rights have been impacted by the decision of a public body exercising a public function. There is no requirement that he demonstrates that the decision directly impacts his business or interferes with his human rights (options B and E are therefore incorrect). Option C is incorrect because the local authority is exercising a public function when it regulates the licensing of taxi drivers in its area.

Did you choose the correct answer?   YES ☐   NO ☐

See *Revise SQE: Constitutional and Administrative Law*, **Chapter 7** for a discussion of this area of law.

A44 of 90 (page 69)   **Area of law assessed: Contract law**

The correct answer was C. This is because specific performance and injunctions are equitable remedies and are awarded at the discretion of the court. If damages provide an adequate legal remedy, then it is unlikely that the court will exercise its discretion and award either remedy when there is sufficient recourse at common law. Specific performance is an equitable remedy and as such it is at the court's discretion, and is not a question of reasonableness (option A is therefore incorrect). Option B is incorrect: it is a clearly inaccurate statement as the purpose of the award of an injunction is to avoid an inequity when there is no adequate remedy at common law. Option D is incorrect because specific performance or an injunction are not confined to contracts for the sale of land and could be awarded in relation to contracts for goods, for example. Option E is incorrect because it is very unlikely that the court would grant specific performance in relation to a contract of service. The effect would be to compel an employee to work and would only be awarded in exceptional circumstances.

Did you choose the correct answer?   YES ☐   NO ☐

See *Revise SQE: Contract Law*, **Chapter 10** for a discussion of this area of law.

A45 of 90 (page 70)   **Area of law assessed: Dispute resolution**

The correct answer was D. This is because the claimant has made the defendant an offer, which they have gone on to beat at trial. Part 36 of the Civil Procedure Rules 1998 states that, unless it was unjust to do so, the defendant will pay the claimant's costs on the standard basis until the expiry of the relevant period (21 days after 1 March, so 22 March) and on the indemnity basis thereafter (therefore option E is incorrect). Split costs orders would only be applicable here if the defendant had made a Part 36 offer which had been more advantageous than the amount the claimant was awarded at trial (therefore, option C is incorrect). Any amounts in respect of interest will be dealt with once the court has made an order concerning the mechanism by which costs wil be calculated (making options A and B incorrect).

Did you choose the correct answer?   YES ☐   NO ☐

See *Revise SQE: Dispute Resolution*, **Chapter 10** for a discussion of this area of law.

A46 of 90 (page 70)   **Area of law assessed: Business law and practice**

The correct answer was E. This is because there is insufficient money in the company to pay all of the money owed to the company's ordinary unsecured creditors. This MCQ requires a candidate to ascertain which of the creditors will have already been paid (secured loans and employees = £383,160,000) and which fall lower down the statutory order of distribution than the ordinary unsecured creditors and are therefore not likely to receive any money on the distribution (loan to person connected to a director). Total unsecured creditors = £71,440,000, therefore there is a shortfall of £33,750,000. This means that option E is the option closest to the amount that best represents the percentage that will be paid to this category of creditors.

Did you choose the correct answer?   YES ☐   NO ☐

See *Revise SQE: Business Law and Practice*, **Chapter 6** for a discussion of this area of law.

A47 of 90 (page 71)   **Area of law assessed: Constitutional and administrative law and EU law**

The correct answer was A. This is because a quashing order quashes the original decision and obliges the authority to retake a decision in a lawful way (e.g. by following the prescribed procedure). A quashing order is therefore likely to be the most appropriate order from the list of orders provided. The court also has the power to make a mandatory order if it wished to compel the local planning authority to do something specific, or do so within a set timeframe (in this case, to consider the planning application and comply with its statutory duty to consult interested parties), but the making of such orders is comparatively rare and is unlikely to be necessary in these circumstances described in the scenario. Options B, C, D and E are incorrect because they identify remedies that would not be appropriate in this case.

Did you choose the correct answer?   YES ☐   NO ☐

See *Revise SQE: Constitutional and Administrative Law*, **Chapter 7** for a discussion of this area of law.

A48 of 90 (page 71)   **Area of law assessed: Tort law**

The correct answer was D. This is because the frequency, location and timing of the lorries would indicate a claim in private nuisance. Option A is incorrect as the period of time the claimant has lived in the area is irrelevant. Option B is incorrect as a claim in public nuisance can only be brought if it affects a class/group of the public; there is no evidence of the wider public being affected. Option C is incorrect as *Rylands v Fletcher* refers to the escape of items that are non-naturally on the land; that is not relevant to this case. Option E is incorrect as the defence of 'coming to the nuisance' will not succeed because the nuisance has arisen following the claimant living at that property; the expansion of the warehouse operator's business has come after the claimant has lived at the property for some time.

Did you choose the correct answer?   YES ☐   NO ☐

See *Revise SQE: Tort Law*, **Chapter 7** for a discussion of this area of law.

A49 of 90 (page 72)   **Area of law assessed: Legal system of England and Wales and sources of law**

The correct answer was A. This is because the statutory provision lists a number of firearms followed by the words 'or other similar weapons'. This means a judge may determine that weapons that are not specifically listed in the section are firearms for the purpose of the legislation (option B is therefore incorrect). Option C is evidently incorrect as the rule of language in option A can be used here. There are strong similarities between air rifles and the other firearms listed in the statute, so an air rifle is likely to be considered to be similar to the other types of firearms listed in the statute (option D is therefore incorrect). The *noscitur a sociis* rule is only applied where the meaning of a word used in the statute is ambiguous or unclear. Option E is incorrect because the *noscitur a sociis* rule would not be applicable to this scenario.

Did you choose the correct answer?   YES ☐   NO ☐

See *Revise SQE: The Legal System and Services of England and Wales*, **Chapter 3** for a discussion of this area of law.

A50 of 90 (page 72)   **Area of law assessed: Tort law**

The correct answer was A. This is because the storage of cannisters past their expiry date is a negligent act, and is likely to do harm if they escaped. Storing the cannisters is a non-natural use of the land. This is a classic *Rylands v Fletcher* example; whilst an explosion alone would not be sufficient, an explosion caused by a negligent act would be. Option B is incorrect because the explosion is not an inevitable accident; it is due to the owner of the building storing gas cannisters past their expiry date. Option C is incorrect as the interference on the and lacks sufficient frequency, which is a requirement for private nuisance. Option D is incorrect as there is no requirement under the rule in *Rylands v Fletcher* that the incident be more than an isolated incident. Option E is incorrect as the explosion has not affected a class/group of the public, and thus public nuisance is irrelevant.

Did you choose the correct answer?   YES ☐   NO ☐

See *Revise SQE: Tort Law*, **Chapter 7** for a discussion of this area of law.

A51 of 90 (page 73)   **Area of law assessed: Constitutional and administrative law and EU law**

The correct answer was B. This is because Parliament is the sovereign law-making body in the UK so no court can declare any statutory provision in domestic legislation void (options A, C, D and E are therefore incorrect). Section 4 of the Human Rights Act 1998 does, however, give the High Court, the Court of Appeal and the Supreme Court the power to issue a declaration of incompatibility. In essence, this power simply allows those courts to declare that they do not consider a statutory provision to be compatible with the rights guaranteed under the European Convention on Human Rights.

Did you choose the correct answer?   YES ☐   NO ☐

See *Revise SQE: Constitutional and Administrative Law*, **Chapter 8** for a discussion of this area of law.

A52 of 90 (page 73)   **Area of law assessed: Contract law**

The correct answer was B. This is because a guarantee creates a secondary obligation, which only arises once the landlord has first pursued a claim against the man. It does not provide a direct cause of action against the guarantor. Option A was incorrect. Whilst this statement is accurate of an indemnity, which does create a primary obligation for the surety to pay the debt of another, it is not accurate in relation to a guarantee. If the terms of the original agreement are unenforceable, then the guarantee is also unenforceable (option C is therefore incorrect). The guarantor is under an obligation to pay the debt once the man has failed to pay the debt and the landlord cannot recover the arrears from the man. There is no requirement for the landlord to wait for the full length of the lease to run in order to make their claim (therefore option D is incorrect). Option E is incorrect because the secondary obligation of the guarantor is for any unpaid amount accrued for the duration of the lease.

Did you choose the correct answer?   YES ☐   NO ☐

See *Revise SQE: Contract Law*, **Chapter 10** for a discussion of this area of law.

A53 of 90 (page 74)   **Area of law assessed: Dispute resolution**

The correct answer was D. This is because, when actively managing the claim, the court must take account of all of the factors involved, including complexity, value and any independent expert evidence needed to assist the court with reaching a determination (therefore options A, B and C are incorrect). This will be done with regard for proportionality (making option E incorrect).

Did you choose the correct answer?   YES ☐   NO ☐

See *Revise SQE: Dispute Resolution*, **Chapter 7** for a discussion of this area of law.

A54 of 90 (page 74)   **Area of law assessed: Dispute resolution**

The correct answer was A. This is because the witness is giving two separate pieces of information to the court with different evidential bases. The evidence of how many pints the defendant drank is direct evidence of what the witness saw. This evidence is admissible as direct evidence. On the other hand, the evidence that the defendant was 'too drunk to drive' is opinion evidence. The witness is not qualified to provide this opinion and the evidence is inadmissible. The witness is permitted to comment on what they saw (how many pints the defendant drank), but is not permitted to comment on the effect that the alcohol had on the defendant. All other options are therefore incorrect.

Did you choose the correct answer?   YES ☐   NO ☐

See *Revise SQE: Dispute Resolution*, **Chapter 8** for a discussion of this area of law.

A55 of 90 (page 75)   **Area of law assessed: Dispute resolution**

The correct answer was D. This is because the test for whether permission is to be granted by the court is that the appeal would have a real prospect of success *or* there is some other compelling reason for the appeal to be heard (making option C incorrect). The prospect of success must be more than fanciful (therefore option E is incorrect) and, whilst the decision of a lower court being wrong is a ground of appeal, we are asked here about the test for whether permission to appeal will be granted (making options A and B incorrect).

Did you choose the correct answer?   YES ☐   NO ☐

See *Revise SQE: Dispute Resolution*, **Chapter 11** for a discussion of this area of law.

A56 of 90 (page 75)   **Area of law assessed: Tort law**

The correct answer was E. This is because if the court considers that the claimant can be financially compensated, and that it would be oppressive to grant an injunction, they will award damages instead. Option A is incorrect as the claim has not been pursued in negligence (and an injunction is not a remedy for a negligent act). Option B is incorrect as the claimant has already established nuisance and succeeded in their claim. Option C is incorrect as the claimant has been successful in their claim. Option D is incorrect as disturbance to a class of people relates to public nuisance, not private nuisance.

Did you choose the correct answer?   YES ☐   NO ☐

See *Revise SQE: Tort Law*, **Chapter 8** for a discussion of this area of law.

A57 of 90 (page 76)   **Area of law assessed: Contract law**

The correct answer was D. This is because the burden of establishing mental incapacity rests with the party raising it. It is also for them to show that the other party knew or ought reasonably to have known about the incapacity. Once proven, the effect of mental incapacity will make the contract voidable. Mental incapacity renders a contract *voidable*, not void (therefore, option A is incorrect). Option B was incorrect because the party claiming incapacity must prove such; it is not for the other party to disprove. Option C was incorrect because the contract is voidable for incapacity and is not automatically set aside. Option E was incorrect because actual knowledge of any incapacity is not required if the man can prove that the other party ought to have known about such incapacity.

Did you choose the correct answer?   YES ☐   NO ☐

See *Revise SQE: Contract Law*, **Chapter 3** for a discussion of this area of law.

A58 of 90 (page 76)   **Area of law assessed: Legal services**

The correct answer was D. This is because the solicitor is entitled to their usual fees plus the additional conditional agreement fee. The solicitor's usual charging rate is £190, and they have undertaken 20 hours of work. They are therefore owed £3,800 plus the Conditional Fee Agreement (CFA) fee. The CFA is set at 25% so the additional fee would be 25% of £3,800 (which is £950). The total amount that the client is liable to pay the solicitor is therefore £4,750 (£3,800 plus £950). Options A, B and C are incorrect because they fail to correctly calculate the solicitor's fee under the terms of the CFA. Option E is incorrect because the client's case was successful, so the client is liable to pay their solicitor's fees.

Did you choose the correct answer?   YES ☐   NO ☐

See *Revise SQE: The Legal System and Services of England and Wales*, **Chapter 8** for a discussion of this area of law.

A59 of 90 (page 77)   **Area of law assessed: Constitutional and administrative law and EU law**

The correct answer was A. This is because decisions of the Court of Justice of the European Union (CJEU) have persuasive effect (rather than binding effect) on UK courts. As such, the Supreme Court may choose to consider the CJEU decision, but it is not bound to follow it. Option E is incorrect because the Supreme Court may refer to CJEU decisions if it chooses to do so. The fact that the CJEU decision relates to the interpretation of EU retained law does not impact the relationship between the CJEU and the Supreme Court (options B and D are therefore incorrect). Option C is not the best available option because it fails to acknowledge that the Supreme Court may refer to CJEU decisions if it chooses to do so.

Did you choose the correct answer?   YES ☐   NO ☐

See *Revise SQE: Constitutional and Administrative Law*, **Chapter 9** for a discussion of this area of law.

A60 of 90 (page 77)   **Area of law assessed: Business law and practice**

The correct answer was C. This is because the Partnership Act 1890 provides for equal apportionment of profits and losses. Therefore, options A, B and E do not represent deviations from the Act. Option D ignores the salary provision.

Did you choose the correct answer?   YES ☐   NO ☐

See *Revise SQE: Business Law and Practice*, **Chapter 2** for a discussion of this area of law.

A61 of 90 (page 78)   **Area of law assessed: Contract law**

The correct answer was D. This is because the postal rule provides an exception to the general rule that an acceptance is only effective when communicated. As the woman's acceptance was posted using Royal Mail, her acceptance will be effective when posted. This is two days after the offer was made and before the watch was sold to the third party. The man therefore breaches his contract with the woman when he sells the watch to a third party on the sixth day. It is correct that the promise to keep the offer open will not be binding in the absence of consideration, but the woman's acceptance is effective before the five days have elapsed and before the watch is sold to the third party (option A is therefore incorrect). Option B is incorrect because the promise to keep the offer open is not binding in the absence of consideration. As noted above, this is irrelevant as the woman's acceptance was effective on the second day when the offer was still open. If properly posted using Royal Mail, the woman's acceptance will be effective when posted. Her acceptance is effective on the second day and when the offer is still open (therefore, option C is incorrect). Option E is incorrect because the postal rule provides an exception to the requirement for the woman to communicate her acceptance.

Did you choose the correct answer?   YES ☐   NO ☐

See *Revise SQE: Contract Law*, **Chapter 1** for a discussion of this area of law.

A62 of 90 (page 78)   **Area of law assessed: Tort law**

The correct answer was B. This is because the employer has a non-delegable duty of care to their employees. Option A is incorrect as the school owes their employees a duty of care. Option C is incorrect as the claimant was not the author of their own misfortune; they tripped over a toolbox carelessly left by the builders. Option D is incorrect because it is unlikely the claimant's damages will be reduced if the contractor's toolbox was carelessly left on the floor. Option E is incorrect as it is reasonable to assume that teachers may attend the school premises during the summer holidays to collect marking.

Did you choose the correct answer?   YES ☐   NO ☐

See *Revise SQE: Tort Law*, **Chapter 5** for a discussion of this area of law.

A63 of 90 (page 79)   **Area of law assessed: Ethics and professional conduct**

The correct answer was D. The is because the SRA Code of Conduct requires a solicitor not to provide or offer to provide any benefit to witnesses dependent upon the nature of their evidence or the outcome of the case. In essence, the SRA Code of Conduct prohibits the payment of witnesses in civil proceedings except for their reasonable expenses for attending court (option A is therefore incorrect). Compensation that goes beyond expenses is not permitted. Option B is incorrect because the solicitor must never offer to pay a witness to give evidence. Whilst option C is correct in part, it is incorrect that witnesses cannot claim expenses. Option E is incorrect because the ultimatum given by the witness does not permit the solicitor to offer payment.

Did you choose the correct answer?   YES ☐   NO ☐

See *Revise SQE: Ethics and Professional Conduct*, **Chapter 2** for a discussion of this area of law.

A64 of 90 (page 79)   **Area of law assessed: Tort law**

The correct answer was C. This is because the claimant and his brother have been estranged for 30 years, and the requirement for a close tie of love and affection can be rebutted with evidence to the contrary. Option A is incorrect as post-traumatic stress disorder (PTSD) is a medically diagnosed psychiatric illness. Option B is incorrect because the claimant arrives minutes after the brother is pronounced dead and he is significantly burnt and disfigured; the claimant therefore did witness the immediate aftermath. Option D is incorrect as the zone of danger refers to a primary victim and the claimant is seeking a claim on the basis that they were a secondary victim; the zone of danger is therefore irrelevant. Option E is incorrect as it is irrelevant whether or not the brother is next of kin.

Did you choose the correct answer?   YES ☐   NO ☐

See *Revise SQE: Tort Law*, **Chapter 3** for a discussion of this area of law.

A65 of 90 (page 80)   **Area of law assessed: Ethics and professional conduct**

The correct answer was E. This is because the SRA Code of Conduct states that a solicitor need not disclose information material to the matter in which the claimant is involved where the information is contained in a privileged document that the solicitor has knowledge of only because it has been mistakenly disclosed. In such circumstances, the solicitor is best advised to return the papers to the correct party and not inform the claimant of the error. None of the other options accurately represent the status of the law and are therefore incorrect.

Did you choose the correct answer?   YES ☐   NO ☐

See *Revise SQE: Ethics and Professional Conduct*, **Chapter 2** for a discussion of this area of law.

A66 of 90 (page 80)   **Area of law assessed: Legal services**

The correct answer was D. This is because the interests of justice test is automatically satisfied for trials before the Crown Court (options A, C and E are therefore incorrect). Option B is incorrect because the client automatically satisfies the test; the likelihood of them receiving a custodial sentence is therefore irrelevant. Option C is incorrect because legal aid is not dependent on the likely outcome of the trial.

Did you choose the correct answer?   YES ☐   NO ☐

See *Revise SQE: The Legal System and Services of England and Wales*, **Chapter 8** for a discussion of this area of law.

A67 of 90 (page 81)   Area of law assessed: Tort law

The correct answer was D. This is because the injuries were not caused by the danger presented by the state of the premises but by the incorrect use of well-maintained premises; the Occupiers' Liability Act 1984 is concerned with trespassers injured 'due to the state of the premises' (this is not the case here). Option A is incorrect because even though the theme park owners know that children may potentially enter the park, and have attempted to do something about that by installing cameras, the injuries are not caused by the state of the premises. Instead, they are caused by the children's incorrect use of well-maintained premises. Option B is incorrect because the court will judge the claimants by the standard of a reasonable 11-year-old child. Option C is incorrect because the injuries have not been caused by the state of the premises. Option E is incorrect as the court is unlikely to find a duty of care existed under the Occupiers' Liability Act 1984 and therefore contributory negligence will not be a factor.

Did you choose the correct answer?   YES ☐   NO ☐

See *Revise SQE: Tort Law*, **Chapter 6** for a discussion of this area of law.

A68 of 90 (page 81)   Area of law assessed: Business law and practice

The correct answer was D. This is because the father is a connected person and the transaction fulfils all other requirements of the definition. The definition of a substantial property transaction from the Companies Act 2006 is: an arrangement under which a director (or connected person) acquires or is to acquire from the company a non-cash asset, or the company acquires or is to acquire from a director (or connected person) a non-cash asset where the value is substantial (ie, exceeds 10% of company's asset value and is more than £5,000 or it exceeds £100,000) and the consideration is cash. If the transaction fulfils this definition, the company needs to approve it by passing an ordinary resolution of the shareholders. If this approval is not obtained, the transaction is voidable. Options A and B are not of substantial value so do not fulfil the definition. Option C is a sale to an employee (not a director or connected person) so does not fall within the definition. Option E describes non-cash consideration so does not fall within the definition.

Did you choose the correct answer?   YES ☐   NO ☐

See *Revise SQE: Business Law and Practice*, **Chapter 4** for a discussion of this area of law.

A69 of 90 (page 82)   Area of law assessed: Contract law

The correct answer was C. This is because the contract is between the retailer and the customer. The retailer in turn has a contract with the manufacturer. The man is not a party to the contract between the retailer and the manufacturer. The man cannot bring a claim against the manufacturer for the breach of contract between the manufacturer and the retailer. Option A is incorrect because the manufacturer is only liable for their breach of contract with the retailer. The man's claim for breach of contract arises as the goods are not of satisfactory quality. This is a breach of condition, which would entitle the man to reject the goods and seek a refund from the retailer (therefore option B is incorrect). Option D is incorrect because there is no evidence of negligence. The goods are not of satisfactory quality and the man should pursue his claim for breach of contract against the retailer. Option E is incorrect because the question is framed based on a claim for breach of contract due to the goods not being defective.

Did you choose the correct answer?   YES ☐   NO ☐

See *Revise SQE: Contract Law*, **Chapter 4** for a discussion of this area of law.

A70 of 90 (page 82)   **Area of law assessed: Tort law**

The correct answer was D. This is because illegality is a complete defence to a claim in negligence. Option A is incorrect as the defence of consent is not relevant because the claimant is performing an illegal act. Option B is incorrect as the defendant did not owe the claimant who was burgling his house a duty of care. Option C is incorrect as the court would have to find primary liability attached to the defendant in order to then consider whether or not the claimant contributed to their injuries. Option E is incorrect as the defendant has a complete defence to the claim.

Did you choose the correct answer?   YES ☐   NO ☐

See *Revise SQE: Tort Law*, **Chapter 4** for a discussion of this area of law.

A71 of 90 (page 83)   **Area of law assessed: Tort law**

The correct answer was B. This is because the assault is too remote from the initial negligence so as to allow the claimant to succeed. Option A is incorrect as the employer has not been negligent in the second incident, which sees the claimant assaulted by a member of the public. Option C is incorrect because the assault is not a direct consequence of the employer's negligence. Option D is incorrect as consent is not relevant as a defence in the scenario. Option E is incorrect as there is no negligence associated with the assault and it is not foreseeable that a change in occupation would lead to the claimant's facial injuries.

Did you choose the correct answer?   YES ☐   NO ☐

See *Revise SQE: Tort Law*, **Chapter 2** for a discussion of this area of law.

A72 of 90 (page 83)   **Area of law assessed: Ethics and professional conduct**

The correct answer was D. This is because the SRA Code of Conduct requires solicitors to act in a way that encourages equality, diversity and inclusion (Principle 6) and must not unfairly discriminate. The trainee solicitor is entitled to practise her religion and dress according to her beliefs (option A is therefore incorrect). A policy that prohibits the trainee solicitor from wearing a hijab could be discriminatory, and is not neutral (option B is therefore incorrect). The best course of action would be for the supervisor to speak to the senior partner on behalf of the trainee solicitor. This approach would avoid causing discomfort or difficulty for the trainee solicitor should they speak with the senior partner personally (therefore option C is incorrect). Option E is incorrect because it is not an absolute right to wear a hijab at work. Reasonable adjustments must be considered by the employer to accommodate the employee's religious beliefs, and whilst it would be unlikely that the law firm would not accommodate such beliefs, there is no absolute right.

Did you choose the correct answer?   YES ☐   NO ☐

See *Revise SQE: Ethics and Professional Conduct*, **Chapter 2** for a discussion of this area of law.

A73 of 90 (page 84)   **Area of law assessed: Tort law**

The correct answer was B. This is because the museum was clear about the fact that it was an event for over 18s only and the child's parent knew this to be the case as they have smuggled their child into the show without the knowledge of the security team. Option A is incorrect on the basis that the museum did not expect there to be any children on the premises. Option C is incorrect as the museum has complied with their duty of care under the Occupiers' Liability Act 1984, and in any event the child was not injured by the state of the premises but due to the fact that they were not being supervised by their parent. Option D is incorrect as trespassers are owed a duty of care under the Occupiers' Liability Act 1984 as long as preconditions are met – this is not relevant here. Option E is incorrect as the museum is unlikely to be at fault due to the fact that the child should have been supervised.

Did you choose the correct answer?   YES ☐   NO ☐

See *Revise SQE: Tort Law*, **Chapter 2** for a discussion of this area of law.

A74 of 90 (page 84)   **Area of law assessed: Constitutional and administrative law and EU law**

The correct answer was B. This is because remedial orders are a type of statutory instrument that is designed to allow the government to quickly amend law in order to remove incompatibility with the Human Rights Act 1998. Remedial orders are not a type of remedy (therefore, option A is incorrect). Option C is incorrect because it states that remedial orders allow the Government to *overturn* legislation, which is not accurate. Option D is incorrect because remedial orders are not a type of bill. Option E is incorrect because the courts cannot *direct* Parliament to do anything; the remedial order simply gives Parliament the ability to amend Acts.

Did you choose the correct answer?   YES ☐   NO ☐

See *Revise SQE: Constitutional and Administrative Law*, **Chapter 8** for a discussion of this area of law.

A75 of 90 (page 85)   **Area of law assessed: Legal system of England and Wales and sources of law**

The correct answer was A. This is because judges may only refer to external aids to interpretation where a word or phrase used in the statute is ambiguous or unclear. Option B is incorrect because it implies that judges may refer to external aids to interpretation whenever they wish, which they cannot. Option C is incorrect because the parties' consent is not relevant to the rules concerning statutory interpretation. Academic literature is a recognised external aid to statutory interpretation; options D and E are incorrect because they imply that academic literature may not be used as an aid to statutory interpretation.

Did you choose the correct answer?   YES ☐   NO ☐

See *Revise SQE: The Legal System and Services of England and Wales*, **Chapter 3** for a discussion of this area of law.

A76 of 90 (page 85)   **Area of law assessed: Business law and practice**

The correct answer was E. This is because option E fails to actually appoint to the office of director – it simply gives the director a contract of employment. All other options describe the process of appointment (with or without a service contract, which is desirable but not essential).

Did you choose the correct answer?   YES ☐   NO ☐

See *Revise SQE: Business Law and Practice*, **Chapter 4** for a discussion of this area of law.

A77 of 90 (page 86)   Area of law assessed: Legal services

The correct answer was D. This is because fixed-fee arrangements tend to be used when a case is relatively straightforward and the solicitor is able to accurately estimate how much time they are likely to spend on the case. In this case, the client's divorce is straightforward and it is highly unlikely that the solicitor would need to undertake any additional work in respect of this matter. For these reasons both the client and solicitor are likely to find a fixed fee to be an appropriate source of funding in this scenario. Options A, B and C are incorrect because these types of funding options are not appropriate in family matters such as divorce. Option E is incorrect as this is not the most appropriate option for a client faced with a straightforward divorce case.

Did you choose the correct answer?   YES ☐   NO ☐

See *Revise SQE: The Legal System and Services of England and Wales*, **Chapter 8** for a discussion of this area of law.

A78 of 90 (page 86)   Area of law assessed: Business law and practice

The correct answer was C. This is because the entrepreneur is a higher rate taxpayer and clearly has other sources of income so all profits are likely to attract income tax at the higher rate of tax for an individual, and with this option the rates payable of corporation tax are lower. Option E is not correct because there are (at least) two people in this business. Options A, B and D would all make the entrepreneur responsible for their share of the profits which would be taxed at the higher rate of 40%. If the profits were made by a private limited company, the rate of corporation tax is 20%. This does not of course allow for the extraction of the profits from the company by the entrepreneur, but this is not required on the facts.

Did you choose the correct answer?   YES ☐   NO ☐

See *Revise SQE: Business Law and Practice*, **Chapter 1** for a discussion of this area of law.

A79 of 90 (page 87)   Area of law assessed: Ethics and professional conduct

The correct answer was A. This is because the SRA Code of Conduct requires solicitors to ensure that the service they provide to clients is competent and delivered in a timely manner, and to maintain their competence to carry out their role and keep their professional knowledge and skills up to date. If the newly qualified solicitor has doubts about their competence, they should decline the task and inform the senior partner. The newly qualified solicitor may need additional training or support if they wish to expand their competence into complex commercial transactions (therefore option B is incorrect). Option C is incorrect because the solicitor has a duty to provide a competent level of service; delegation to non-qualified legal staff is not appropriate. Option D is incorrect as the solicitor has an obligation to act in a timely manner and asking for an extension of time is not appropriate. Option E is incorrect because the newly qualified solicitor may have competence in other aspects of the retainer, and it would not be in the client's best interests for them to cease to act.

Did you choose the correct answer?   YES ☐   NO ☐

See *Revise SQE: Ethics and Professional Conduct*, **Chapter 2** for a discussion of this area of law.

A80 of 90 (page 87)   Area of law assessed: Legal services

The correct answer was E. This is because it is likely that this behaviour would amount to harassment under the Equality Act 2010. Harassment occurs when a person is subjected to unwanted conduct that relates to certain protected characteristics, in this case sexual orientation, and the unwanted conduct violates the victim's dignity, or creates an intimidating, hostile, degrading, humiliating or offensive environment for that person. Options A, B, C and D are incorrect because they fail to classify the conduct as harassment.

Did you choose the correct answer?   YES ☐   NO ☐

See *Revise SQE: The Legal System and Services of England and Wales*, **Chapter 6** for a discussion of this area of law.

A81 of 90 (page 88)   Area of law assessed: Dispute resolution

The correct answer was B. This is because disclosure on the standard basis requires that all documents relevant to a claim, whether or not they adversely affect a party's case, are disclosed (making options A and C incorrect). Option D is incorrect as past representations have no bearing on the duty to disclose, and option E is incorrect as this is not an order for specific disclosure.

Did you choose the correct answer?   YES ☐   NO ☐

See *Revise SQE: Dispute Resolution*, **Chapter 9** for a discussion of this area of law.

A82 of 90 (page 88)   Area of law assessed: Contract law

The correct answer was C. This is because the fire occurred after the contract was formed and was beyond the control of either party. It is now impossible to perform the contract. This will frustrate the contract for the hire of the concert hall. The effect of frustration is to discharge the parties of any future obligations under the contract. Any obligations that arose before the frustrating event are not affected by the frustration. Option A is incorrect. If the requirements of frustration are met, then the parties will not be bound by their strict contractual obligations. Option B is incorrect because there is no evidence of any negligence on the facts; the fire was the fault of neither party. As noted above, the effect of frustration is to discharge only those future obligations under the contract. The parties are not discharged of all obligations under the contract (therefore option D is incorrect). Option E is incorrect as the effect of frustration is to discharge future obligations under the contract, meaning the music promoter will not have a valid claim for damages.

Did you choose the correct answer?   YES ☐   NO ☐

See *Revise SQE: Contract Law*, **Chapter 9** for a discussion of this area of law.

A83 of 90 (page 89)   Area of law assessed: Tort law

The correct answer was E. This is because the court will only reduce damages for contributory negligence and there has been no effect to the claimant's injuries due to the lack of a seatbelt (therefore there has been no such contribution). Option A is incorrect as the claim will succeed due to the fact that the defendant was negligent and collided with the vehicle at the roundabout. Option B is incorrect as there would only be a 25% reduction for contributory negligence if the claimant had suffered injuries that could have been avoided by the use of a seat belt. Option C is incorrect as there would only be a 15% reduction for contributory negligence had the claimant been wearing a seat belt. Option D is incorrect as there has been no break in the chain of causation.

Did you choose the correct answer?   YES ☐   NO ☐

See *Revise SQE: Tort Law*, **Chapter 4** for a discussion of this area of law.

A84 of 90 (page 89)   **Area of law assessed: Dispute resolution**

The correct answer was A. This is because it is the claimant's responsibility to prepare the trial bundle (making option B incorrect), which must incorporate all of the documentation that both the claimant and defendant will be relying upon in the trial (making option C incorrect). Options D and E are incorrect as the court will have already considered proportionality of evidence relating to value of the claim at case management stage, and have decided on whether they need to intervene to limit the volume of documents that the defendant is seeking to rely upon.

Did you choose the correct answer?   YES ☐   NO ☐

See *Revise SQE: Dispute Resolution*, **Chapter 11** for a discussion of this area of law.

A85 of 90 (page 90)   **Area of law assessed: Legal services**

The correct answer was B. This is because the nominated officer (NO) is under a legal duty to make a Suspicious Activity Report (SAR) to the National Crime Agency (NCA) as soon as is practicable. Options A and C are incorrect because they imply that the NO is under a duty to make a disclosure/SAR to the Solicitors Regulation Authority. Options D and E are incorrect because they imply that the NO is under a duty to make a SAR to the Financial Action Task Force Authority.

Did you choose the correct answer?   YES ☐   NO ☐

See *Revise SQE: The Legal System and Services of England and Wales*, **Chapter 6** for a discussion of this area of law.

A86 of 90 (page 90)   **Area of law assessed: Business law and practice**

The correct answer was A. This is because the client must first satisfy its obligations to HMRC before it can issue dividends to shareholders. Option B, whilst correct, does not provide the full picture of the transaction (ie, the client must first pay its tax liability). Option C is not correct because dividends do not have to be declared by the board (the use of the word 'must' in the distractor demonstrates this). Options D and E are incorrect in law as they do not represent an accurate statement of the process of declaring dividends.

Did you choose the correct answer?   YES ☐   NO ☐

See *Revise SQE: Business Law and Practice*, **Chapter 4** for a discussion of this area of law.

A87 of 90 (page 91)   **Area of law assessed: Constitutional and administrative law and EU law**

The correct answer was D. This is because section 3 of the Human Rights Act 1998 deals with the court's duty to interpret legislation in a way that is compatible with the Convention rights. Options B and C are incorrect because they state that section 2 of the Act deals with this duty. Option A is incorrect because it states that the duty requires courts to interpret legislation in a way that is compatible with the Convention rights. This is not an accurate statement of the duty because the duty only requires the courts so far as it is possible to do so to interpret legislation in a way that is compatible with the Convention rights. Option E is incorrect as it fails to account for the duty imposed on courts by the Human Rights Act 1998 when interpreting legislation.

Did you choose the correct answer?   YES ☐   NO ☐

See *Revise SQE: Constitutional and Administrative Law*, **Chapter 8** for a discussion of this area of law.

A88 of 90 (page 91)   **Area of law assessed: Legal system of England and Wales and sources of law**

The correct answer was B. This is because there are certain presumptions that a court presumes are implied in a statute. The legislation in question deals with criminal offences. The court would presume that any criminal offence requires proof of mens rea unless the statute expressly states otherwise (options A and D are therefore incorrect). There are no presumptions relating to when the legislation will come into force (therefore, Option C is incorrect). There is, however, a presumption that statutes will not apply retrospectively. Option B is therefore the best answer available. Option E is incorrect because the court would have to determine on a case-by-case basis how the statute has altered the common law, if at all.

Did you choose the correct answer?   YES ☐   NO ☐

See *Revise SQE: The Legal System and Services of England and Wales*, **Chapter 2** for a discussion of this area of law.

A89 of 90 (page 92)   **Area of law assessed: Business law and practice**

The correct answer was B. This is because it is the best option for the client's situation. The MCQ asks what is the 'least likely' manner of dilute control. The use of 'least likely' is designed to test you; 'least likely' indicates that it is possible that all options may dilute control, or risk such, in some way. For example, whilst preference shares do not generally carry voting rights, it is possible that such shares could contain voting rights. For that reason, option A (and the other options) are evidently not the correct answers. Option B is the only option which does not, in some way, divest any element of ownership (and thus voting rights) to a third party.

Did you choose the correct answer?   YES ☐   NO ☐

See *Revise SQE: Business Law and Practice*, **Chapter 4** for a discussion of this area of law.

A90 of 90 (page 92)   **Area of law assessed: Legal services**

The correct answer was D. This is because the client intends to pay their legal fees through a travel insurance policy that includes some cover for legal costs. This type of funding is known as before-the-event (BTE) insurance (options B and C are incorrect as they refer to after-the-event insurance). The client also intends to pay any additional legal fees from their own funds. This is known as a private retainer. The client therefore intends to fund their cases through BTE insurance and a private retainer (options A and E are incorrect as they only include one funding option each, as opposed to both funding options). Only Option D correctly identifies the correct types of funding.

Did you choose the correct answer?   YES ☐   NO ☐

See *Revise SQE: The Legal System and Services of England and Wales*, **Chapter 8** for a discussion of this area of law.

Your results

Now add your scores for Session 1 and Session 2 together, and award yourself an overall mark and percentage for *Prepare for SQE1: FLK1 Practice Assessment*.

Your total score for Session 1:	_____ / 90
Your total score for Session 2:	_____ / 90
Your total score for FLK1:	_____ / 180
Percentage:	_____ %

■ PASS MARK

The pass rate for the FLK1 assessment is only set following the FLK1 assessment; there is no fixed pass mark.

According to the SRA Marking and Standard Setting Policy, the pass mark is determined by the SRA Assessment Board through the Modified Angoff method. This method involves a panel of qualified solicitors familiar with Day One competence which reviews each question and predicts how many out of ten just-competent Day One solicitors would answer the question correctly. A summary and average of the rating for each question by each member of the panel produces a cut score.

Further statistical processing based on the actual performance of the candidates and to correct for measurement errors is then carried out to arrive at a final pass mark for the assessment. The pass mark for the SQE will vary between different sittings of the assessment, to ensure that the standard of the assessment remains consistent from one sitting to the next.

For this reason, it is not possible to prescribe a pass or fail result based upon your performance to *Prepare for SQE1: FLK1 Practice Assessment*. The SRA has provided information based upon previous sittings of SQE1 to assist your understanding of the likely pass mark, contained in Table 5.

Table 5: Pass mark and rate of FLK1

Date of SQE1 Assessment	FLK1 pass mark	FLK1 pass rate
November 2021	57% (103 correct answers)	67% (out of 1084 candidates)
July 2022	56% (101 correct answers)	64% (out of 1899 candidates)
January 2023	57% (103 correct answers)	59% (out of 3103 candidates)
July 2023	53% (96 correct answers)	66% (out of 3647 candidates)

You can access the statistical breakdown for subsequent assessments on the SRA (sqe.sra.org.uk) and Revise SQE (revise4law.co.uk) websites.

If you are scoring over 50%, it is likely that you can feel prepared for SQE1. If you are scoring below 50%, you are advised to revisit some of the FLK subjects where you feel less confident. However, please note:
- Only **you** can decide **if** you feel adequately prepared to sit SQE1.
- Only **you** can decide **when** is the appropriate time to sit SQE1.

Remember: passing this practice assessment does not guarantee that you will pass SQE1. Do not be complacent, and remember to ensure that you are fully prepared by using all resources available to you.

You can use the companion volume, *Prepare for SQE1: FLK2 Practice Assessment*, to test your knowledge in preparation for the second SQE1 assessment.

Final words and FAQs

We hope that you found *Prepare for SQE1: FLK1 Practice Assessment* to be beneficial in your preparation for the real FLK1 assessment.

■ FINAL WORDS

Whilst reflecting on your performance in this practice assessment, we advise the following:

- Review your answers to the practice questions carefully. If there are any MCQs that you answered incorrectly, consider whether you need to return to one of our *Revise SQE* guides to consolidate your understanding and knowledge. If you answered an MCQ correctly, do not become complacent; stay on top of your knowledge and understanding.
- Review your approach to answering MCQ-style questions. Use the guidance at the start of every *Revise SQE* guide, and the advice in the Introduction of this book to assist you.
- Review your preparation for sitting a closed-book timed assessment. Consider how you best retain large amounts of information, and whether you need to consider a different approach to retaining information. If nerves got the better of you, what could you do to mitigate this in the future?

The team at *Revise SQE* wish you the best of luck in your SQE1 assessments.

■ FREQUENTLY ASKED QUESTIONS

Below are a number of FAQs that you may have about SQE1. If you have a question not considered below, please get in touch with the team via our social media channels where we will endeavour to answer your questions.

1   **Do I need a degree to sit SQE1?**

    Whilst you do not need to have a degree (law or otherwise) to sit the SQE1 assessments, you cannot be admitted as a solicitor without a degree or an equivalent qualification.

2   **Do I have to undertake an SQE-preparation course?**

    You are not required to undertake an SQE-preparation course in order to undertake the SQE1 assessments. However, if you wish to consider an SQE-preparation course, visit the Revise SQE website at revise4law.co.uk for a list of providers.

3   **When do the SQE1 assessments take place?**

    From 2023, SQE1 sittings will take place on a regular pattern of two SQE1 sittings per year: January and July. The SRA aims to start each SQE assessment in the third week of the relevant month. Dates will be published 12 months before the relevant assessment. The SRA is likely to introduce additional sittings in the future.

4   What are the SRA rules on verifying my ID?

When you register for the SQE, you have to provide a valid, official photo identification. You will need to upload an image of your ID when you register, to allow the SRA to authenticate it and verify your identity. Suitable ID includes a passport or photocard driving licence. The SRA recommends using a passport.

5   What ID is required on the day of my SQE1 assessment?

You must bring two forms of ID with you to both of your SQE1 assessments – a 'primary' and 'secondary' form of ID:

- The primary form of ID must include a photograph of you (eg, a photocard driving licence or passport).
- The secondary form of ID must contain your full name and signature (eg, a signed debit or credit card).

The SRA warns that if you fail to present the correct forms of identification, you will be denied entry to the examination and forfeit your examination fee. Furthermore, the name on your ID must exactly match the name you provided when you registered with the SQE.

6   Are reasonable adjustments available for SQE1?

Under the Equality Act 2010, the SRA has an obligation to make reasonable adjustments for any person who has a disability. Whilst all candidates must be assessed against the Statement of Solicitor Competence and the Statement of Legal Knowledge, and must reach the Threshold Standard to qualify, reasonable adjustments will be made to ensure that candidates with disabilities are not disadvantaged.

It is the responsibility of the candidate to identify that they require reasonable adjustments when they register for the SQE1 assessments, and supporting evidence is required. Reasonable adjustments are determined and afforded on a case-by-case basis, but can include additional time and breaks, a separate room, a reader and many more. The SRA has published a guide on reasonable adjustments for SQE on their website (sqe.sra.org.uk).

7   Is there a dress code for sitting SQE1?

There is no dress code for SQE1. You can wear what you feel comfortable in, but you may be asked to remove bulky external clothing during security checks. You are advised to wear sufficient layers of clothing to ensure you are comfortable, depending on the room temperature at the test centre.

8   What if something happens during the assessment?

Following the SQE1 assessment, if you feel that something has happened that could affect your performance during the assessment, you can submit a claim for 'mitigating circumstances'. These include:

- a mistake or irregularity in the administration or conduct of the assessment
- evidence of bias in the conduct of the assessment
- subject to the Fit to Sit Policy and SQE Assessment Regulations, a candidate's illness or other personal circumstances beyond their reasonable control, which have materially and adversely affected their marks or performance in the assessment, or are likely to.

Disagreement with the academic judgment of the assessors cannot amount to mitigating circumstances.

9   When do I find out about my results in the real SQE1 assessment?

You will get your results approximately 5–6 weeks after sitting SQE1. The SRA will send you an email notifying you that the results are available in your SQE account. Results will only be posted within your account on the SQE website and will not be sent out to you. You will be able to save them as a PDF.

10   What do I get when I receive my results for the real SQE1 assessment?

For each FLK assessment, you will receive information about the date of the assessment, the date of the transcript, the attempt number of that sitting, the pass mark for that FLK (expressed as a percentage), your mark for the assessment (expressed as a percentage), your quintile score (ie, where you are placed in your assessment, in comparison to everyone else who took the assessment with you) and your result (ie, whether or not you have passed).

11   What is a quintile score in SQE1?

Candidates are afforded a quintile score as part of their results for SQE1. Your quintile score tells you how you were placed in comparison to other candidates sitting the SQE. This score is likely to be relevant to employers. There are five categories:
- 1st (top) quintile candidates – the top 20% of performers
- 2nd quintile candidates – the next 21–40%
- 3rd quintile candidates – the next 41–60%
- 4th quintile candidates – the next 61–80%
- 5th quintile candidates – the final 81–100%.

12   When can I book SQE2 assessments?

Unless you have an exemption from sitting SQE1, you cannot book SQE2 until you have received your results for SQE1. Similarly, you cannot book to resit an SQE1 assessment until you have received the results for your previous attempt at that assessment.

13   How many attempts do I get at SQE1?

You will only be allowed three attempts at both FLK1 and FLK2. These have to be taken within six years from the first attempt of an SQE assessment. The clock starts from the first day of the first assessment you sit. If you fail FLK1 and/or FLK2 three times during this six-year period, you must wait until that six-year period expires before reapplying, and previous passes will not be carried forward.

14   Can I retake an assessment I have passed?

You cannot resit an assessment you have passed to improve your marks, under any circumstances.

15   Do I have to pass both FLK1 and FLK2?

In order to pass the SQE, you must pass both SQE1 and SQE2. SQE1 consists of two exams, FLK1 and FLK2, and you must achieve the necessary mark in both to pass SQE1 as a whole. If you fail either FLK1 or FLK2, you are only required to resit the assessment that you failed. You must also pass both SQE1 and SQE2 in order to apply to become a solicitor.

16 If I fail an assessment, do I have to pay a resit fee?

Yes, a fee is required if you have to resit either FLK1 or FLK2. The full SQE fee is required if a candidate has to resit both FLK1 and FLK2. The current resit fees are available on the SRA website.

17 Can I appeal if I fail SQE1?

Yes, there is a process for appealing against the decision of the Assessment Board. Any appeal must be made on one of the recognised grounds, and must be made in writing via the Appeals Form which is available in your candidate account. A fee is required to be paid to submit an appeal; this fee is refundable if your appeal is upheld. The SRA has published an Appeals Policy, available on its website.

Jean Khoury

A Letter to the Pope

Table of Contents

Chapter 4: A Model For Renewed Spiritual Formation: The School Of Mary's Experience _____ 57

Chapter 5: The "Solid Foundations" Course: A Practical Illustration _____ 67

Chapter 6: Reforming Spiritual Theology? _____ 79

Chapter 7: Reforming Theology, A Call For Deeper Engagement _____ 87

Chapter 8: Transfiguration Of The Church _____ 99